Japanese Folktales

by N. Muramaru

YOHAN PUBLICATIONS, INC.

JAPANESE FOLKTALES

First printing July 1992

Copyright © 1992 by Norikazu Muramaru

Illustrations Cover: Tatsuo Isoya
            Text: Kasama Seisakushitsu

published by

YOHAN PUBLICATIONS, INC.
14-9 Okubo 3-chome, Shinjuku-ku, Tokyo, Japan

Printed in Japan

Contents

~ messages of excerpt

Japanese Folktales

The fountain
of youth

IN the West there are many tales about the "Fountain of Everlasting Youth," such as Ponce de Leon and Fernando de Soto searching for the fountain several hundred years ago to keep people young and gay in Paradise.

Here in this country (Japan), there are similar stories from olden times. This is one of the many folktales told and retold among the people in the western part of the province of Tohtohmi, in what is now Shizuoka Prefecture.

Once upon a time there was an old man, with fluffy gray hair, living peacefully with his wife in a lonesome village by the mountains. The old man usually went into the mountains to gather firewood to make their living.

One day early in the morning he went to work in the nearby mountains, while his old wife stayed at home to do the daily housekeeping. After a time

1

evening approached, when he usually came home with a bundle of firewood on his back, but that day he did not come home.

The old woman was a bit worried, to think what might have happened to her aged husband in the mountains. However, there was nothing she could do, as they were living all alone apart from the rest of the villagers. As she was deep in thought, imagining what could have happened to the old man, she heard a rustling noise outside.

She hurried out of the house to see what might be the noise, and there she saw a dark shadowy figure coming toward her. When she perceived the outline of a man carrying a bundle of firewood on his back, she was very much relieved, and she began to walk to meet the dark figure. As she came nearer she strained her eyes and peered closely into his face.

"Why it's you! But what made you come so late? Now, hurry, it's cold out here, come, come...," so saying she dragged her reluctant husband into the house.

When they were inside the house, she cried out in astonishment, "What! Is this you! Why have you dyed your hair so black to make you look so young? I can't believe you! Oh! I can't believe you!"

And then she began to weep even more sorrow-fully.

"Now, listen, my dear. You must believe me...," said the man.

Then he told her that when he went into the mountains and began to gather firewood as usual, he felt thirsty, but there was no water nearby. So he climbed up a beautiful mountain and came down to the foot of it on the other side, where he found a refreshing spring. There he quenched his thirst.

"But when I took a drink, it was like 'sake' wine, so I took several more drinks. Then I began to feel sleepy, and slept into the night. When I awoke I felt so fresh and strong ... I guess it's the spring water that made me so young."

While the old-man-turned-young man was relating his story the old woman listened very carefully with much curiosity. Then she said cheerfully.

"Why, if that is the case, I must go there tomorrow to drink the water, because I, too, want to become young."

"Yes, yes. You'd better go, because it's no good for me to be the only one becoming young."

So the next morning the old woman went into the mountains, as told by her young husband, to look for the spring that could make her young. The man, of course, stayed at home to look after the house for her.

Evening came, but she did not come home. This time the man began to worry, and he stayed awake throughout the night waiting for her to return. But she did not come home, even after the sun had risen.

Therefore, he decided to go into the mountains to look for her. He clearly recalled the path to the wonderful spring, so he reached it easily. There he expected to find her, but she was nowhere to be found.

While looking around the clear spring, he suddenly heard a faint muttering noise nearby. He carefully followed the noise, and when he reached the spot, he saw a baby wrapped in a big kimono, wriggling and about to cry.

"Is it you, dear?" asked the man softly but sharply, bewildered, recognizing the kimono the old woman had worn the day before when she went into the mountains.

To this the baby nodded slightly and muttered feebly, "The water of the spring was so sweet, that I drank too much of it, and see what has become of me."

Zen dialogue

ZEN is a kind of Buddhism characterized by self-contemplation and meditation, and by a kind of catechism, in which questions and answers are exchanged between two persons who test each other's wit and intelligence. This is one of many stories.

Once upon a time the chief abbot of the Zen headquarters in the city of Kyoto decided to go to the country to test the qualifications of the priests in different temples under his supervision. He began in the Province of Tamba in the north of Kyoto.

After visiting a number of smaller temples, he found that most of the country priests were unqualified to remain in charge of their temples, so he expelled them and ordered them to do some more studying in the capital.

When the bonze of a small temple heard that the great Zen master was coming from the capital to test him, he was very upset because he had grown old and had forgotten many things due to lack of study.

"Ah, what shall I do when the great master comes to me?" he said.

There was a little sweet shop by the gate of the temple. Here all kinds of rice cakes, incense and flowers were sold to the parishioners who came to visit and worship at the temple. The shopkeeper, like all others in his trade, was a very affable man, but he was also very cunning. When he heard that the bonze of the temple was in trouble, he went to the temple to see if he could be of any help.

"My dear man, you are a mere shopkeeper and you have no idea how difficult it is to solve Zen problems. All you can do is to be good to me until the day I am expelled from this temple. Ah, Great Buddha, please give me all your wisdom for the day the great master from Kyoto comes to me. When the 'dialogue' is over I shall return it to you."

"My dear Bonze, if you are so afraid to meet the great master from Kyoto, why don't you let me meet him? I have a lot of common sense and I may be able to answer some of his questions."

The two men, who were old friends, talked the

situation over for some time. They finally decided that the shopkeeper would don the bonze's robe and meet the great master from Kyoto.

The next day the great Zen master from Kyoto came to the little country temple. As previously arranged, the shopkeeper dressed up in the bonze's robe and came out to meet the Zen master.

When they sat down facing each other for the verbal bout, the master made a little circular sign with both fingers of his hands in front of him, which in Zen means, "What is your wisdom?" The shopkeeper, of course, had no idea of this but without losing a moment, he formed a large circle with both of his hands. The great master appeared well satisfied with the answer.

Then the master showed his index finger, right in front of the shopkeeper's eyes, which in Zen means, "What or how are you?" To this the shopkeeper, without waiting a moment, replied with five of his fingers. Thus he showed that he was quick of mind, which is one of the prime requisites in this kind of exchange of questions and answers.

Again the great master nodded with contentment. After a little thought, he showed three fingers, which in Zen signifies the three things worthy of respect — the Buddha, his teachings and his disciples. To this the shopkeeper quickly responded by pulling the most exaggerated faces he could think of. He even stuck out his tongue and made the biggest eyes he could with his fingers.

When the master saw these faces he murmured, "I am beaten," and lowered his head in acknowledgement of his defeat. On seeing the master yield, the shopkeeper all of a sudden flung his mace at the master's head.

The great master was, of course, thunderstruck, but he could not complain, as he had already admitted defeat. He hurriedly left the temple.

But the man who was most astounded was the bonze, who had been stealthily watching the two men engaged in this decisive Zen dialogue.

"Why, my dear man, I did not know you were such a learned man. Where did you get all your Zen knowledge?"

"Ah, what a time I had!" the shopkeeper chuckled. "When the great master asked me if my rice cakes are as small as this with a small circle, belittling and disgracing my rice cakes, I told him they are as large as the heavens. I did this by making a bigger circle with both of my hands. Then he showed me one finger, asking me how much I sold them for. I answered that they are five coppers each. So far there was nothing that hurt me, but when he tried to bargain me down to three coppers by showing three fingers, I got so mad that all I could think of was to make faces at him. And when he admitted he was wrong and apologized by lowering his head I could not hold my temper any longer, so I gave him a crack on the skull with the mace."

The bonze could say nothing, and the two lived as the best of friends thereafter.

The cherry tree of Ankokuji temple

THERE is an old Buddhist temple called Ankoku-ji in the city of Ayabe, not far from the former capital of Kyoto. Many old temples and shrines in Japan have strange tales, which are told and retold over the years. The story, which is written in its records, is about a cherry tree that used to grow in the temple compound.

One spring morning hundreds of years ago, a gardener came to this temple. He was a friend of the priest. He was carrying a beautiful cherry sapling.

"Good morning, Abbot. How are you today?" asked the gardener cheerfully.

"Ah, good morning. What have you got for me today?" For whenever the gardener came to the temple he always had something to sell to the priest.

"Today I have a splendid cherry tree that could be a treasure to this temple."

"Let me take a look at it," said the priest, who was very fond of garden trees.

The gardener proudly took the cherry sapling from his basket and placed it before the priest.

"Hmmn, it looks like a fine sapling," the priest whispered and admired it from different angles. He continued to examine the sapling for some time. Finally he muttered, "A fine tree."

The gardener watched intently how the priest reacted to the tree with which he expected to make a big profit, as he had on other occasions. At long last, the priest asked, "How much do you want for it?"

The gardener could not overlook the priest's satisfaction, and decided to make even more profit than he had planned before coming to the temple. He answered, "Ten gold pieces."

"What! Ten gold pieces! That's exorbitant! Be more sensible, my dear man," the priest shouted. "No, no. That is too much, I can't accept your price."

"But my dear Abbot, if you are so satisfied with it, ten gold pieces are nothing compared with the pleasure you will get out of it," the gardener retorted.

"Of course, I am satisfied with it, but ten gold pieces are far too expensive."

"If that is your decision, I have nothing more to say. I must find some other place where this sapling will be appreciated," the gardener replied coldly and began to pack it away.

"Wait! Just a moment! You must be more sensible, you must understand how I stand here."

"Yes, but this is good for ten gold pieces anywhere in the country."

"Well, if you are so determined, let's do it this way. I will give you five gold pieces right on the spot. How about it?" the priest begged.

"What! Five! No! I have just told you that it is ten and nothing less. You can't find a tree better than this anywhere."

"Now, listen"... and so they continued to argue the matter over. Finally the gardener decided to pack up his wares and go. But all of a sudden he gave a scream of fear. Slowly, as if forced, he knelt down and finally squatted on the ground. He could not speak, even though he had his mouth open.

"What's the matter?" And the astounded priest knelt down to see what had happened to the gardener. To his astonishment, he saw that the roots of the cherry sapling had extended themselves and were coiled tightly around the gardener's legs.

At length the gardener came to and pleaded with the priest, "Dear Abbot, please recite your sacred sutra and get these roots away from my legs. Then I will confess the truth."

As the priest was reciting a holy sutra of the Great Buddha, the roots of the cherry sapling gradually loosened and the gardener was freed. Then the gardener confessed that he had purchased the cherry sapling for only one gold piece from a neighboring nursery.

As a result, the gardener learned to be honest. It is said that the cherry sapling was planted in the compound of the temple and flourished there for many, many years. (From the old records of An-kokuji temple, Ayabe, Kyoto Prefecture.)

The fox and the old man

O<small>NCE</small> upon a time there was an honest old man who lived all alone in a mountain hamlet. He was very fond of flowers and his garden was filled with flowering plants.

One day he went to the nearby mountain to gather firewood. After he had collected enough, he started home along the hilly road. He happened to find a pea on his way home.

"Ah, if I leave it here it will die, but if I plant it in my garden it will grow and give me a whole lot of peas," he thought. "Yes, yes, I will plant it in my garden."

He brought it home and planted it in the garden. Although the weather was rather chilly, within a few days it began to sprout, and before long it bore plenty of peas.

The old man was very happy to see the pea grow so large, and said, "Ah, this is what I had expected.

The peas are ready and I will pick them tomorrow and have a good meal."

He went to sleep early that night, but toward midnight he was woken by some rustling noises in the garden. When he peeped through the window, he saw a fox eating the peas. In a towering rage he jumped out of the house with a sickle and chased after the mischievous fox. After a scuffle, he finally got the better of it.

"Darn you! I will kill you for that ...," he said panting, and he lifted the sickle high ready to thrust it into the fox's throat.

But the fox pleaded, "Before you kill me, listen to me. I will make you a rich man and then you can kill me ..."

After a while the old man nodded, thinking it was not a bad idea, and he kept the fox in a pen until all its bruises and wounds had healed. When the fox was well enough to walk, it called the old man and said, "I am well and strong enough to walk. Now take me to the village market and sell me, and you will make a lot of money."

As soon as it had said the magic words, the fox transformed itself into a handsome steed. On seeing the steed before him, the old man cried out in astonishment. "What witchcraft! Sure enough, I will become the richest man in the village, if I can only sell it."

And he led the steed to the village market. He had no difficulty in finding a customer and he sold the steed for a good price.

Several days passed, and the fox came back to the man. "Master, what do you want me to become next?" it asked. The old man thought for a moment, then he patted the fox lightly and said.

"This time become a fat milking cow." And sure enough within a few seconds a splendid cow stood before him. The old man proudly took it to the village market and sold it for an enormous price. He was so elated that he spent the next few days doing nothing but counting his money and gorging himself on delicious food.

Several days passed and the fox came back to the old man again. "What do you want me to be next?" the fox asked. "A teakettle. That is easy to sell."

"That is not difficult. Just watch me," answered the fox obediently and changed itself into a sizeable teakettle.

As on the other occasions, when the old man brought it to the market, he had no difficulty in

finding a customer. But this time the customer was a cautious man, and he said, "It looks like a good one, but if there is a hole in it, it might leak. Let me fill it with water, put it over the fire and boil it."

So they made a fire together and began to boil the kettle. The old man was very anxious because he knew the fox would not be able to stand the fire for any length of time. But the customer put on more firewood, and the fire became stronger and stronger. Finally the old man could stand it no longer and said, "Don't you think that is enough?"

Just as he was about to put out the fire, the tea-kettle swelled up and burst loudly.

The fox, of course, died, and the old man was badly scalded by the hot water that burst out of the teakettle.

And so ends the story of the fox and the old man.

Ichiemon the fisherman

A long time ago there was a fisherman called Ichiemon. There was nothing special about him, except that he was fond of sake (rice wine). He loved it more than any other fisherman in his neighborhood.

Although he was a strong drinker, he was not an alcoholic. He knew how to drink and when to stop drinking. Sometimes he got dead drunk, but even then he never caused trouble with his drinking friends, so he was known as a jolly drinker.

As soon as he got out of bed in the morning, the first place he went was the pantry where there was a keg of sake. After breakfast he went to his boat moored at the quay with a big bottle of sake. It was his habit to take a drink or two before he started to row to the fishing bank.

One evening he went out fishing, as usual taking with him a bottleful of sake, hoping to get a big haul. It was a beautiful night with thousands and thousands of big and small stars glittering in the sky above. In addition the sea was calm, like the water of an inlet.

"What a wonderful night, and who can resist a drink or two?" he muttered as he gurgled down a mouthful of sake, admiring the nocturnal serenity above him.

And then he lowered his fishing line into the water. For a long time there was no bite from the fish down in the sea.

"What's the matter with the fish? Are they sleeping? Of course, it's night. I can be wrong sometimes," he said to break the solitude, and to comfort himself.

"Well, I can wait, you know, until morning, too. Hmm, let me have another shot," he whispered, fearing he might scare the fish. And then he gurgled down another mouthful of sake.

The quietude of the night seemed to continue indefinitely.

As Ichiemon had nothing to do but wait for the fish to bite, he kept on sipping sake, when he suddenly felt the boat lurch. "Am I drunk?" he thought and begun to look around to see whether he had become dizzy.

As he was nearer to the stern, he had to peer toward the helm to see if there was any wave that might have shaken the boat. While he was straining his eyes through the starlight, he thought he saw someone hanging onto the side of his boat in the water.

"Who are you? And what are you doing there?" he cried out softly, to see whether there was anyone there.

There was no response for a while, but by this time Ichiemon was quite sure that there was a living being staring at him. A few moments passed, and quite suddenly Ichiemon lightly tapped his knee and shouted in a low but distinct tone:

"Where have you come from, you Kappa?"

To this the kappa (water imp) quietly replied, "Ichiemon-san, please give me a drink of your sake."

"What did you say? Give you a drink? No! No! Sir! This is my sake. If you don't get away, I'll crack the dish on your head," Ichiemon yelled and threatened to throw an oar.

The next moment the water imp scampered away noiselessly into the water.

In the meantime he went to sleep, having had too much sake. When he woke up from a chill running down his spine, he was lying on a sandy beach.

"What! Where am I? Am I dreaming?" Ichiemon the fisherman jumped up and sure enough he was standing firmly on a sandy beach. He could vaguely see his boat floating not far away in the sea beyond.

After completely regaining himself he lost no time and started to swim toward his boat. When he reached the boat, he found a kappa sleeping with the sake bottle as a pillow. He was mad with anger and wanted to kill it, but as he watched its innocent face his wrath gradually subsided. When the kappa awoke from its long slumber, it said:

"Ah, Ichiemon-san, I'm very, very sorry I drank all your sweet sake. Please forgive me this time, I'll never do it again, and from now on I'll do anything for you." The kappa prostrated itself flat in the boat, quivering all over its body for its misbehavior.

Ichiemon looked at the poor thing for some time, but being a good man he decided to overlook its misdemeanor saying, "All right, all right. Go ashore and fill the bottle with sake, and I'll let you go."

The kappa looked puzzled, then it said, "That's impossible. Nobody will sell sake to a kappa like me."

"Then what can you do to atone for your misdeed?"

"Well, I can do a lot of things for you. Since you are a fisherman, every time you come around here, I'll give you a good catch of fish for the day."

Thereafter, every time Ichiemon went fishing he came back with a big haul, much to the envy of his fellow fishermen.

And every time he went to the fishing bank, he never forgot to pour a small portion of his sake from the bottle into the sea, saying, "Hey, Buddy, I hope you know how I feel."

The gambler and the goblin

ONCE upon a time there was a hapless gambler. Every time he went gambling he was sure to lose, and one day he lost everything and was stripped naked, except for his loincloth.

"Now, I must do something; I can't go home and face my wife like this," he muttered as he trekked despondently into the nearby forest. At length he came to a big tree, under which he sat down to rest. As soon as he was seated comfortably on the soft grass, he instinctively went into the posture of throwing the dice, as if he were in a gambling house.

"Ah, come Edo (Tokyo) … there you are … Now, come Osaka … fine … wow!" the gambler began to shout after throwing his dice before him, with the most exaggerated gestures, as if he were really caught up in a game. This mimicking act continued for some time.

"Hey, young man, what are you so excited

24

about? Can you really see Edo and Osaka?" someone asked in a low reverberating voice behind him.

Taken by surprise, the man turned around to see who it was. When he saw the being, he felt his heart stop beating and not a muscle would move. A giant, long-nosed goblin was standing, staring curiously at him.

"Ah, don't get excited. I'm not going to eat you. I'm only interested whether you can really see Edo and Osaka," the goblin said quietly trying not to upset the man any further.

"Aha," the gambler thought, after regaining himself, but his mouth was so dry that he could not speak. After a minute or so he finally managed to say very faintly, "Yes, yes, you can really see . . . see what you want with this pair of dice."

"Really? If so, please sell them to me," the goblin demanded eagerly.

Although the gambler was very afraid of the goblin, and thought himself to be in mortal danger, he decided to take a chance.

"No, I can't part with these dice. They are the most valuable treasure I have. But what can you give me for them? I might change my mind," the gambler said.

"Well, let me see … if they are so valuable, how about my sedge hat and mantle?"

The gambler knew that the goblin's sedge hat and mantle could make one invisible. "Fine, if the goblin really means what he says, I'll be the luckiest man in the world," the cunning gambler thought, and immediately exchanged his two dice for the sedge hat and mantle.

After the gambler got them into his hands, the first thing he did was to go to the village wine-shop, wearing the sedge hat and mantle, and drink as much rice wine as he could. And the next place he visited was the tailor, where he stole a suitable kimono to dress himself properly.

The goblin, on the other hand, was furious at being cheated by the cunning gambler, and vowed to take revenge on him.

When the gambler reached home, his wife was out, so he hid the sedge hat and mantle in the inner part of the closet and went to sleep. It was late in the morning when he woke up the next day. As he started to go out, he remembered the goblin's miracle hat and mantle, and looked into the closet, but they were not there.

"Surely I swear I put them in here last night,"

he said to himself and asked his wife about them.

"Ah, my dear, they looked so dirty and miserable that I decided they were useless, and I burned them in the backyard," his wife said.

The gambler had no time to scold her, and rushed out into the backyard, hoping he might be able to rescue them. But all he found there was a pile of ashes.

"Ah, what luck," he said, totally crestfallen. But the next moment something flashed into his mind, and then he quickly began to smear the ashes all over his body. "This will make me invisible. Let me try it at the village market," he said to himself and walked over to the market. There he picked up various morsels to eat, but nobody seemed to notice him.

"Fine, I'll try the wineshop," he nodded triumphantly, and walked toward the shop. As he was walking, a light shower fell on him, and he put up his hands to protect himself.

Fortunately the wineshop was not crowded. The gambler stealthily walked up to the counter and stole a drink when the master was not looking. But when he tried to steal another drink, the master saw a vague, shadowy hand taking away a cupful of rice wine, and as he continued to follow the cup, it tilted and emptied in midair about a yard away.

"Darn that fox," the master mumbled hatefully, thinking it was a fox playing one of its usual tricks, so when the wine cup came back, he grabbed the shadowy hand by the wrist and twisted it as hard as he could.

"Ouch!" the gambler cried out, but it was too late. He had not realized that the rain shower had partially washed the ashes from his hands.

And they still enjoy telling this story in the village wineshops in that northern country, today known as Aomori Prefecture.

The ghost of
Kogenji temple

A long time ago in the Kojiyamachi section of the
city of Nagasaki, down south in Kyushu, there was
a small, rusty sweet shop catering mainly to the
children in the neighborhood.

One night very late after the master of the shop
had closed his doors, he heard a soft tapping from
outside. At first he doubted his ears, but when he
heard it a second time he reluctantly rose and went
to the front door to see who could be disturbing
him so late.

When he opened the door he saw a young woman, dressed in a whitish kimono, standing all
alone in the dim darkness. A cold shiver ran down
his spine. He thought he saw a ghost standing
before him.

The woman looked young and beautiful, but her
hair was loose, pluming down softly over her
shoulders. For a moment the master felt dazed and

29

could not find words to say anything, but soon he realized that he must greet her somehow.

"What can I do for you?" he asked to recompose himself and stay his fear.

"Will you be good enough to give me some taffies?" she said in a typical Kyoto accent, not so commonly heard in Nagasaki, and extended her hand, on which was a copper coin with a square hole in it.

The master felt quite relieved, and wrapped three pieces of taffy in tissue paper and gave them to her. The woman received them with a light smile, and soon disappeared into the darkness.

The following night about the same time after the master had closed his shop, the woman came again, bought some more taffies, and vanished quietly into the darkness. On the third night, when the same thing happened the master began to suspect the midnight customer.

"If she is going to scare me every night, I must do something," he thought, but he could not decide what to do. However, when she came for the sixth time, the master finally determined to find out why a young and beautiful woman should come and buy taffy so late at night.

And so he persuaded the more adventurous and daring young men of the neighborhood to shadow her if she came for a seventh time to buy taffy. While they were waiting the woman appeared from the darkness, but her attitude was somewhat different.

"My dear Master, I have no money tonight. By the benevolent blessings of the Great Buddha, please favor me with some taffies," the woman pleaded sorrowfully.

"Ah, don't worry, don't worry. Here are the taffies with the blessings of our Great Buddha," said the master gladly and gave her the sweets.

When the woman started to leave, the master and several young men also began to follow her. After rounding a number of street corners, the woman walked into the Buddhist temple of Kogenji, and when she reached the graveyard behind the temple, she suddenly faded away in front of a newly erected grave.

All the men following her stopped and looked at each other, as if to ask whether they should go near the grave, but while they were hesitating they began to hear a weird cry nearby. They all listened intently straining their ears, then someone whispered.

"It's a baby."

When they reached the new gravestone, sure enough, they could hear a baby's cry. They notified the abbot of the temple. When the gravestone was removed, they found the baby in the coffin with a woman the abbot had buried some days ago.

"So it was," the abbot sighed and nodded several times, while mumbling a short sutra, as if consoling the spirit of the dead woman, and told them the following story.

It was in May in the 5th year of Enkyo (1748 A.D.) that a sculptor called Fujiwara-Kiyonaga, who was one of the parishioners of the temple, returned from his studies in Kyoto. While Kiyonaga was in Kyoto he fell in love with a woman, but he left and returned to Nagasaki alone. As soon as he was back in his native city he got married to a local girl. In the meantime, the woman in Kyoto could not forget Kiyonaga and so she came to Nagasaki, but after she was told of Kiyonaga's marriage, she got so disappointed and broken-hearted that she consequently died. When Kiyonaga heard of her death, he felt so sorry that he asked the abbot of Kogenji temple to bury her there, placing the customary obituary gift of six copper coins in the coffin, her

fare to cross Sanzu-no-kawa, the River Styx in Japanese mythology, in the other world.

About a month after the incident, an apparition appeared by the bedside of the sweet shop master saying, "My dear Master, I wish to thank you for all the kindnesses. I am happy Kiyonaga has adopted my baby boy. Now I want to repay you for them. If there is anything I can do for you ..."

Although the man was half asleep, he managed to say, "We are always short of water in summer, so if you can give us water in summer, that is all I wish to ask you."

Several days later the man discovered a new well near his house, which after more than 250 years still gives refreshing water all the year round. Today it is called the "ghost's well" by the people of Nagasaki.

As for Kiyonaga, he later became a leading sculptor, made a life-sized replica of his beloved woman from Kyoto in clay as a lasting memory of her and donated it to Kogenji temple. Even to this day it is on display to the public, as one of the rare treasures of the temple on the 16th day of August every year on the occasion of the Bon Festival, or the Buddhist All Souls' Day.

The crabs of Kanimanji temple

ONCE upon a time there was an honest farmer, living peacefully with his daughter in a little village called Kabata in the Province of Yamashiro, south of Kyoto. He was a very devout follower of the Goddess of Mercy, which was the main deity of worship in the village temple. The daughter was, like her father, also an ardent believer in the same goddess.

One day while she was walking along the bank of a nearby stream, she happened to see a group of children catching crabs in the water. She felt sorry for the crabs, so she gave a few coins to the children and told them to return the crabs to the stream. The children were happy to get some money and quickly threw the crabs into the stream.

Several days later when her father was returning from his work for the day, he happened to come across a snake about to swallow a frog in the rice paddy.

35

"Wait!" he cried out. "For Buddha's sake, don't kill the frog!"

On hearing him scream the snake hesitated, and since the man seemed so terribly excited the snake waited for him to calm down. At length the man came to himself, but he could not think of anything to appease the snake. He knew he had no time to lose, lest the snake seize the frightened frog, so he hurriedly said, "If you will spare the frog's life, I will give you my daughter as your wife. . . "

When the snake heard him it slowly turned away from the frog, and slid into the nearby grassy bush.

"Ah! What a frightful thing I have said," the man gasped. "How shall I explain this to my daughter?" and he worried over the unfortunate incident with the snake all the way home.

When he reached home he was so upset that he looked extremely tired.

"Why, father, what is the matter with you? You look so weary and tired," the daughter asked.

But the old man could not tell her the truth, so he just said that the day's work had been heavy and that it might have been the hard labor.

"Then you must go to sleep as soon as supper is finished," she replied tenderly.

That night the man could not go to sleep. He tried to think of all the possible ways to get away from the snake, but there was nothing he could do before the morning came.

The next day, before the farmer started for the fields to work, a high court noble appeared at the farmer's house. The farmer received him very respectfully, but realized instantly that he might be the snake transformed into a human being.

"I have come to take your daughter, as you have promised," the nobleman said haughtily.

As the man was not yet prepared to give his daughter to the snake, he asked for three days to prepare his daughter properly to be a bride, saying, "You may come on the evening of the third day, and your promise shall be fulfilled."

In the meantime he called his daughter, and told her all about the snake and the poor frog, but she was not upset. She said, "Let us go to the temple and ask the priest what advice he can give us to face the situation."

And so they went to the temple, and asked what they might do with the evil snake.

"Since you are both devout followers of the Goddess of Mercy, my advice would be to recite the most holy Buddhist sutra to the Goddess, and I am sure you will receive the blessings of the Great Buddha. Now, go home and build a small chapel with the strongest wood."

And so the farmer went home and began to build a chapel in his garden, which took him three days. And toward evening the daughter was locked inside, where she began to recite the holy sutra. As soon as the daughter was inside the chapel, the farmer also locked himself up in his house, and waited for the snake to come. Soon afterward the snake, in the guise of a high court nobleman, appeared before the house.

"Here I am to take your daughter. Please give her to me as you have promised."

When the farmer heard the snake's demand, he cried out from his house, "My daughter is now in the small chapel there, and you may take her, as you wish."

Then the snake-man walked over to the chapel, but since it was locked he could not open it. The snake-man began to rap heavily on the sides of the chapel, trying to break the little structure. Since he could not break through, he returned to the form of a giant snake. Then it coiled around the little chapel and tried to crush it with all its might.

Throughout the night the snake strained its body against the small chapel, trying to break through, while the daughter kept on reciting the holy sutra for help from the Goddess of Mercy, which her father heard faintly in his house.

Toward dawn, all of a sudden the terrible noise of the angry snake in the rainstorm ceased. Everything became quiet. Only the faint recitation of the holy sutra could be heard from inside the chapel.

When the farmer went outside to see what had happened, to his surprise he found the snake lying dead in a pool of blood. He also saw innumerable crabs biting its body and dozens of other crabs lying dead beside it.

In this way the daughter was saved by the blessings of the Goddess of Mercy. And the people were so awestricken by the merciful benevolence of the Great Buddha that they built a temple there to worship as a sacred place.

The people later named it Kanimanji temple, in memory of the crabs.

The fated life

ONCE upon a time a beggar happened to walk into a tiny wayside shrine in the country. And he took shelter underneath the porch. While he was dozing he thought he heard someone talking, and opened his sleepy eyes to look around. However, it was still dark, far from the first cock of the morning.

"I'm sure there was someone around," he thought as he gave a big yawn. Just then someone walked up the steps near the place where he was lying down.

"My dear Myojin, dear Myojin," a voice came from the darkness.

"So, this shabby shrine must be for the Myojin deity," the beggar thought.

"Yes, yes. Who can you be tapping at my door so early in the morning? Ah, the god of the mountain. Won't you please come in?"answered Myojin-sama, as this god was known among the villagers.

"No, I can't. I have no time. A baby is being born at the village master's house today. Will you go and see it with me?"

"Too bad, I can't, because I am waiting for a client on an important matter."

After that the first god walked away into the darkness. While the beggar was wondering what to do next to get away from the place without being noticed, the first god came back, and reported to Myojin-sama.

"Thank you, thank you for your trouble. And how was it?" Myojin-sama anxiously said.

"The baby is a boy."

"How long is he going to live?"

"Seven years."

"And how is he going to die?"

"He is destined to die in a flood near his house on the 11th day of the 11th month."

After that the two gods parted. Then the beggar thought, "What a strange conversation," and at the same time he felt a shiver running down his spine.

He hurried to the village master's house. When he arrived at the house, there was a big celebration going on, as the master was overjoyed to have a son, who would in time succeed him to retain his power and authority in the village.

Even the beggar was given such lavish treatment that he began to reconsider how he should tell the happy man that the newly born baby could only live for seven years.

"No, I can't tell him about it on such a happy occasion. That would be too mean for words, even if the story is true." And so the beggar left the house without telling anyone about the baby's fate.

Many years passed, and one day the beggar happened to come to a place which he thought he had seen some years before. While he was fast going over his past memories he gradually began to recall the incident at the lonely wayside shrine and the strange conversation between the gods in the early morning hours about a newly born baby.

"That's right, if I am not mistaken it was here that I heard about the village master's boy, who would only live for seven years, and die in a flood." He then counted the number of years he had roamed in other parts of the country, and it came out to be exactly seven. And more strangely that day was the 11th day of November.

"No. I can't lose any time, I must go to the village master's house and warn him."

Then he hurried to the master's house, and related

all about the strange conversation he had heard seven years before. At first the master could not believe him——but since he was so sincere and serious, he finally agreed to take all the necessary precautions for the boy.

"Yes, my boy went fishing to the nearby river, and if your story is true, he will be drowned there. We must hurry."

The beggar and the master with all his men-servants ran toward the river, and when they reached the bank, they saw the boy walking fee-bly and downcast. They were frightened; the boy looked so pale they thought he was a ghost.

"Why, my son, what is the matter?" the father cried out eagerly.

"Father, today while I was fishing, a water imp came up from the water, and challenged me to a bout of wrestling," he gasped and crumbled on the grass.

"Did you win, my boy? Did you overpower him?" the father asked, very much worried.

"No, I told him that I was hungry. My stomach was empty and I had no strength to wrestle. But if I ate the sweet rice cakes which I had brought for my lunch I could wrestle with him, I told him.

And I began to eat the sweet rice cakes. Then the rascal imp came over and took one, and it was so good that he ate all the rest of the rice cakes."

"And do you know what he said? 'Usually I wrestle with anyone disturbing me over my den in the water. I challenge him to wrestle with me and after knocking him out I carry him into the water. Today, you gave me such good and sweet rice cakes I think I'll spare your life,' and he sank deep into the water."

And thereafter it became a custom of the villagers to make sweet rice cakes on the 11th day of the 11th month, and throw them into the river to appease the water imps so that they might not drown their children.

Mano Choja

It was in the middle of the 8th century, when the country was prospering in the reign of the able Emperor Koken and when the statue of the Great Buddha was erected in Nara, then the capital of the country, that this story begins.

There was a beautiful princess called Tamatsu-hime living in the capital. She was fortunate in every respect, having been able to get everything she had ever wanted. There was nothing in this world that she could not get.

And yet when she came of age, she was suddenly taken ill, and before long blue-black spots of various sizes like birthmarks began to appear all over her body. In time, half of her face was covered with these ugly marks, and she could not go out of the house.

Although she spent most of her time in the house, one day she decided to visit the nearby Miwa-myojin shrine to pray: "O my merciful god, please help me to take away these blotches and make me happy again. If you cannot take away these blotches, please advise me how I must live from now on."

She kept on praying at the shrine every day, hoping to get a favorable answer some day, and after many weeks, one day she finally heard the god's benevolent words:

"Your prayers have been heard. There is only one way to heal your ailment. There is a young man named Kogoro living deep in the mountains of the faraway Province of Bungo (present Oita Prefecture) making charcoal. He is honest and sympathetic, so if you become his wife, in time your markings will disappear, and you will enjoy happiness and wealth the rest of your life."

Tamatsu-hime felt thrilled and thanked the god most reverently, and although she felt very uncertain about finding her way to such a faraway land beyond the sea, she resolved to venture on the quest all alone.

After many weeks of dangerous voyage across the Inland Sea, Tamatsu-hime finally came to the strange Province of Bungo. Thereafter, she started for the deep mountains, which lay beyond the village of Mie, as told by the oracle in Nara. When she reached

Mie, the people told her that Kogoro lived in the mountains, and that it would take a woman like her two days to reach him.

"What a place I have come to," she wept sorrowfully, "but I cannot go back now." So she gathered all her strength and finally reached Kogoro's makeshift hut, almost exhausted.

"My dear man ...," Tamatsu-hime, upon seeing the charcoal man, told him all that had happened to her in the past, and humbly asked him to take her in.

Kogoro was completely taken by surprise to see a woman asking for mercy and entreating him so fervidly to take her as his wife. At first he thought she was a ghost trying to lure him in the guise of a woman, because all he could see of her were her sparkling eyes, as she hid most of her face with the sleeve of her kimono.

He became afraid of the strange woman and finally said, "Whatever the Myojin god of the capital told you, nobody here ever said anything of you to me. Why must I take you as my wife?"

"My dear man, it is the divine oracle of the god in Nara, and I must stay here with you. Please have mercy on me, and let me serve you as your servant.

I will do anything for you," the woman said and began to weep.

Kogoro was puzzled. He did not know what to do, but finally decided to trust everything to fate, and accept her, because he did not have the heart to chase her away.

In this way, Kogoro was forced into a new life with a strange woman with birthmark-like blotches all over her body. Tamatsu-hime, on the other hand, had to adjust herself to her new surroundings, which were more miserable than she had expected. Kogoro's hut was small and dirty, and there was almost nothing in it, so the first thing she thought was to buy things for their new life.

"My dear man, here are two gold coins. If you will go to the village you can buy lots of things. We need some rice to start with, then a cooking pot, a blanket, vegetables and rice bowls, and you can buy whatever other necessities you think are needed," Tamatsu-hime said to Kogoro and sent him to the village below.

Kogoro had never seen a gold coin before. He did not know how valuable it was. While he was walking toward the village he came upon a pond. There were two mandarin ducks swimming there.

"If I catch them, I can have a big party with the woman," he thought and stealthily approached the ducks. When he came very near he threw one of the gold coins like a stone at the ducks, but it missed them, so he threw the other after it. But the ducks flew away and escaped.

Kogoro returned to his hut totally crestfallen, and when he related the incident with the mandarin ducks to Tamatsu-hime, she told him about gold and its value.

"If what you say is right, there are plenty of golden stones in the upper reaches of the valley not far away from here," Kogoro told her.

The following morning they went into the valley and found a whole trove of golden stones. There was a small pond nearby bubbling with hot water. When Tamatsu-hime stuck her hand into the hot spring to pick up a gold stone, she saw the birthmark-like spots on her hand fade away.

Thus, all her marks were washed away by the hot spring water, and Kogoro became the richest man in the Province of Bungo with the beautiful Tamatsu-hime as his wife. Because of his vast riches, he came to be known as Mano Choja. And this all happened more than one thousand years ago.

The buckwheat field miracle

ONE sunny afternoon in early autumn when Shinkichi and his wife were sowing buckwheat seeds in their hilly field, they saw a number of people hurrying toward them from the other side of a hill. When they came nearer, two Europeans, wearing black cloaks, were running at the head of a group of several men and women.

"Please help us, please help us. We are being chased by the authorities, and if we are caught, we will be killed," the elder of the two men said to Shinkichi while panting heavily.

Shinkichi and his wife were rather surprised, because they could not see what it was all about. When he regained himself Shinkichi said, "We are just farmers. We can't do anything against the authorities. If we do things against their wishes, we, ourselves, will be punished. We're sorry, but we can't do anything."

Then one of the foreigners quickly said in faltering Japanese, "If you help save us from the authorities, the Almighty God will surely help you."

Upon hearing him Shinkichi thought that he might be one of the missionaries, but then he also thought he might be one of those foreign traders in Nagasaki running away from the authorities for having done something unlawful.

"If you cannot help us, please don't tell the authorities that we've passed here. We're going down this cliff to hide in one of the caves by the sea," an elderly farmer pleaded, clasping his hands before him as if in prayer.

There was a high cliff just beyond the field, dropping perpendicularly down to the blue sea, which had several large caves in its side.

"You said you are being chased by the authorities. Then you must be some sort of criminals. If we help criminals, we will also be punished. That we cannot do."

"No, no. We are not criminals. We are Christians. So far we have evaded the government agents at Tororo, Fukae and Takahama, but someone must have betrayed us and informed them here," another farmer said sadly.

"If you're Christians, then go down that cliff over there. You'll find several deep caves, where you can hide for a time," Shinkichi's wife advised the fugitives.

"Thank you. Just tell the government agents what you have seen, and we'll take care of ourselves," the Christians said and hurried toward the cliff beyond the field.

"Good," Shinkichi said. "If the government agents come this way, I'll tell them exactly what I have seen. Then they will not be able to suspect me, and they will never find the fugitive Christians, because the cliff is too dangerous, and they won't dare go down it."

A short while later Shinkichi saw a large number of government agents coming toward him from the other side of the field. He became very upset and wanted to stop them from further pursuit. Just as they neared the field, although Shinkichi and his wife had only just finished sowing the seeds, the whole field suddenly burst into blossom, covered with whitish buckwheat flowers in full bloom. Shinkichi was struck with amazement.

The government agents soon reached the place, where Shinkichi and his wife were standing stupefied at the sight of the white buckwheat flowers. And one of the agents, who seemed to be the leader, asked them harshly.

"Hey, farmers! Did you see two foreign missionaries running past here? Which way did they go?"

Shinkichi's mind was blank, but he managed to answer him. "Yes, sir. They passed here while we were sowing the buckwheat seeds. Two foreign missionaries and five or six farmers. They went toward the seashore beyond."

"What! What did you say? While you were sowing the buckwheat seeds?"

"Yes, sir. Exactly, while we were sowing the seeds," Shinkichi repeated.

"Are you sure? Look at the white flowers. You must have sown the seeds some time ago."

"Yes, sir. While we were sowing the seeds," Shinkichi repeated again.

"Enough of your nonsense. That must have been a long time ago. Fellows, we must have mistaken the road. Let's go back, and try the road to the other side of the island," the disgruntled leader said. The party left Shinkichi's buckwheat field as fast as they had come.

When the government agents disappeared beyond the hill, the white buckwheat flowers suddenly disappeared like an illusion, leaving only the barren field as before.

On seeing this, Shinkichi and his wife looked at each other in total awe, then they knelt down to pray to the Almighty God for saving the fugitive Christians.

"My dear Shinkichi, I have seen with my own eyes the miracle of the Almighty God, and now I am convinced that the Christian God will surely save those who are in need. I must now apologize for doubting the Almighty God," Shinkichi's wife said very meekly and continued to pray for a long time with her husband.

Word of this miracle soon spread from one village to the next and in time everybody in the Amakusa Island came to know about it. Thus more and more people were converted to the Christian faith, so an old tale still tells us from Amakusa in Kumamoto Prefecture.

The dream

THIS is the strange story of a young wife, who was so affectionately in love with her husband that even when he went on a journey she could not, for a moment, forget about him.

There was once a young couple, a carpenter and his wife, living very peacefully together in the mountainous part of the village of Hakui, facing the Japan Sea in the southern part of the Province of Noto.

One year the carpenter, called Kichibei, got a job in the faraway city of Edo (present-day Tokyo), then the bustling seat of the military government, in the eastern part of the country.

"If you get friendly with the womenfolk in Edo, I won't stand for it," the wife coyly warned her beloved husband.

"Nonsense, I'm going to Edo to work. Don't be silly," Kichibei said, lightly eluding her childish jealousy.

When he left the wife stood forlornly before their house until her husband finally disappeared over the mountain pass in the distance. There was no news of him for several months, but one day a fellow carpenter suddenly returned to the village. The wife was elated. She went to him to see whether there was any news of her husband, because there was a rumor circulating that Kichibei was living with a woman in Edo.

"Ah, Kichibei is a nice guy. Don't worry, don't worry, he's getting along all right," he said meaningfully, with a sympathetic glance at the anxious wife.

"And ... how does she look?" she asked timidly.

"Well, it's better you know nothing about that. If he's so fickle, why don't we become ...," he teased her and grabbed her by the arm.

The wife slipped away from him, as if she were escaping from something unclean, and when the man approached her again, she spat in his face. There was a fierce hatred in her eyes.

That night she could not sleep, thinking about her husband living so happily with the woman of Edo. It was well past midnight, but her thoughts were wandering in the vast emptiness of the dark night. It must have been when she heard the first cock of the early morning that she found herself wandering in a wide, open grassy field. Then she saw something moving on a distant mound. When the moving object came nearer she saw it was two foxes, a male and a female, romping around and frolicking with each other.

Suddenly she began to chase them, and in time she caught the male fox. She sat astride it, and looked intently at it. The fox's face gradually changed into that of her husband's. She was astounded, but she would not move.

"So, it was YOU, after all," she whispered sharply, squeezing out every syllable with burning hatred from the bottom of her throat.

The man hugged her tightly. His eyes were closed. Then he muttered a woman's name ever so fondly, a name the wife had never heard before. More hatred ran through her, and before long she found her hands choking him, with her long black hair firmly twisted around his neck.

It was on the 11th day of the seventh month in the second year of Meiwa (1765) when the wife decided to go to Edo to see what might have happened to her husband after such a foreboding dream.

It was when she came to the famous Zenkoji nunnery in the Province of Shinano that she saw a woman in traveling attire coming from the direction of Edo, carrying an urn in the customary plain wooden box. Although she was walking with her head bent down as if in deep mourning, she appeared clean and meek. She was beautiful.

As they passed each other, the wife happened to look at the wooden box. To her surprise she read the familiar characters "Kichibei" and a few other smaller words written on the box.

"Ah!" she cried out.

After they had made themselves known to each other, the woman from Edo confided, "Yes, this is Kichibei the carpenter. He died, writhing in agony during the early morning of the 11th day of July, as if he were being strangled and tortured by someone. I have decided to deliver his remains to you as my last duty to him. Now, you can punish me as you wish," she said, repenting deeply.

The two women then became nuns, thinking that the coincidence of their meeting at the Zenkoji nunnery was the benevolent wish of the Great Buddha. And then they went on a mendicant tour of the country to raise funds to make a bell in Kichibei's memory.

The bell still tolls mercifully in the belfry of the Hozai-in temple of Shirase in Ishikawa Prefecture. Today it is known as the "Demoness Bell" by the local people.

The Ishiteji temple

Mᴏʀᴇ than one thousand years ago, there was a man called Kono Emonsaburo. He was the local magistrate of the Ebara district in the old Province of Iyo in Shikoku. As he came from the mighty House of Kono, governor of the Province of Iyo, he was haughty and arrogant. Above all he was mean to the people.

One of the main duties of Emonsaburo was to collect taxes, mostly in the form of rice. As he was cold and heartless, the people abhorred him and ran away from him whenever they saw him walking in the district.

For his spiteful conduct, he was widely known as "Oni Saburo," or Saburo the Devil. He had no conscience, and boasted of his ability to amass riches through illegitimate means, often instigating his henchmen to resort to atrocious practices against innocent people.

One day a strange mendicant bonze, poorly dressed but with seeming dignity in his personality, came to the front entrance to Emonsaburo's residence and began to recite the usual invocation, holding an iron bowl for alms. By this time it was almost second nature to Emonsaburo to take things away from people by force, and the idea of bestowing charity on other people did not occur to him. Thereby, when he saw the frugally clothed bonze, all he could think of was to chase him away.

"No, get away from my house. This is no place for you! Get out!" he shouted.

The bonze must have been surprised at such an abrupt refusal, which he was not used to, as people had all been good to him in the past. He looked up toward Emonsaburo in surprise, and reluctantly walked away. The next day he again appeared at Emonsaburo's residence and chanted the same Buddhist invocation for alms, but he was chased away like the day before.

This continued for eight days, and on the eighth day Emonsaburo was so mad that he grabbed a bamboo broom and took a swipe at the bonze's head. The bonze parried the blow with his iron bowl. When the broomstick hit the iron bowl, it cracked into eight glittering pieces and disappeared in the air. The next moment the bonze himself also faded away and there was nobody before Emonsaburo.

"What?" he cried out in astonishment. "So, the bonze must have been a ghost."

Now, Emonsaburo had five sons and three daughters. A few days after the bonze had disappeared, the eldest of the eight children was taken ill, and to everyone's surprise he died the following day. In the same way, all of Emonsaburo's other children were also taken away from him forever.

"What can this be? Why should I suffer like this?" he said to himself and began to reflect on all that he had done to other people.

Then he came to realize, "Yes, I must have incurred the wrath of the Great Buddha, who had come to admonish me in the form of that bonze, whose iron bowl I cracked into eight pieces."

About the same time, all the people were talking of an itinerant bonze and the new enlightening teachings of the Great Buddha. "He must be Kobo Daishi, the living Buddha, who can deliver us from all evils and lead us into a more sacrosanct world," the people said in high praise of the strange bonze.

When Emonsaburo heard about this he said, "I must see him and beg his pardon for all my misdeeds of the past."

And so he gave all his money and everything he had to the people, and started out on a pilgrimage to search for Kobo Daishi. He continued his journey around all the temples in Shikoku for many years tirelessly, but all his efforts were in vain. Many more years passed and in time he grew older and older.

In the 8th year of Tencho (871 A.D.) after Emonsaburo had been in search of Kobo Daishi over twenty years, he found himself almost senseless from exhaustion at Shosanji temple in the Province of Awa. He was accosted by a kind and sympathetic voice.

"Saburo, Saburo ... I am here, the bonze you have been looking for."

Kobo Daishi caressed the dying Emonsaburo forgiving him of all his past sins and gave him a small stone on which was written "Emonsaburo." Emonsaburo died clenching this stone in his right hand, hoping to be reborn into this world again to do good deeds to the people.

Many years passed, and one year a baby boy was

born to Kono Yasutoshi, governor of the Province of Iyo. He was named Yasukata. At birth his left hand was tightly closed, very much to the wonder of the people of the Kono family. Thereby, the learned abbot of the nearby Anyoji temple was consulted. After reciting a sacred Buddhist sutra, he succeeded in opening the baby's hand. There was a small stone inscribed with "Emonsaburo."

Everybody present was awestruck. Then the abbot decided to change the name of Anyoji to Ishiteji, in commemoration of the birth of a child with a gem-like stone in his hand. (Ishi means stone and te means hand.)

Today after more than one thousand years, Ishiteji has become one of the most flourishing among the 88 temples dedicated to Kobo Daishi in Shikoku.

The challenge

A long time ago, there were two noted sculptors living in Osaka. One was called Myogaya Seishichi and the other was Kusabana Heishiro.

The former always thought that he was much more skillful than the latter, and the latter likewise always thought he was by far the superior of the former. They frequently argued about whose works were better, but they eventually came to realize that they would get nowhere just by talking.

And so one day Heishiro called on Seishichi. "Hi, Seishichi. You know, the townspeople always flatter us two as the successor to the immortal sculptor Hidari Jingoro, but they do not know which of us is better than the other. Wouldn't it be an idea for us each to make our masterpieces and let the towns-folk judge them to decide which of us is more talented?"

To this Seishichi concurred saying, "Fine. That's

a wonderful idea. Let's complete our masterpieces in one month's time from today and ask the people to judge them."

When the townspeople heard about this challenge by their most controversial sculptors, they hailed it as a great event and waited eagerly for the result.

Now, Seishichi was famous for his human figures and other representations of living beings, while Heishiro was talented at depicting flowers and flowering plants.

Since Heishiro had started this challenge he went straight to his workshop and devoted his full time to making what he hoped to be one of his greatest masterpieces. Seishichi, on the other hand, seemed to take things easy and began to spend most of his time visiting the nearby wineshop.

"Why, look at Seishichi drinking his time away. He isn't as serious as he ought to be. How can he ever win the challenge?" some of the more talkative townspeople began to whisper about him.

"Maybe he is contemplating some idea while drinking, for all you know. Some of the more talented artists often devote more time to meditation than to the actual physical work, you know," some others retorted to defend Seishichi's drinking sprees.

On the night before the day to present their masterpieces for public review, Seishichi finally went into his workshop to tend to his work. When it was completed, well after midnight, Seishichi quietly stretched himself and muttered softly:

"Yes. I guess this will do."

When morning came the townspeople gathered in great numbers at the public hall of the town. The works of the sculptors were displayed there for their appraisal. While the people were waiting in suppressed anticipation to see what the two sculptors would present, Heishiro appeared with his assistant, carrying a box. Then he opened the box and took out a beautiful peony flower, which looked like a real blossom.

"Wh ... Woo ...!" and all kinds of praising exclamations were heard from the people.

"Yes. It's an exquisite work, and nobody would believe it's an artificial piece," many of the townspeople said, praising it highly.

While they were admiring the peony flower, Seishichi appeared empty-handed. When he came in front of Heishiro's peony, he put his hand into the sleeve of his kimono and took out a small, blackish object. He placed it beside the beautiful flower.

"What! A rat!" some of the onlookers shouted in amazement.

"Is Seishichi sane? You can never compare a beautiful flower with a rat. Let's hear Seishichi's excuse," some of the more anxious people began to attack Seishichi.

Just then a cat came out of the crowd, and before anyone could stop it, it jumped on the rat and started to run away. All the people were taken by surprise, and the cat scurried under the veranda with the rat in its mouth.

After the cat had run away with the rat, one of the people loudly said, "The bout is won by Seishichi, because his rat was mistaken for a real rat by the cat. If Seishichi's rat were not as real as that, the cat would have remained under the peony flower to rest," another townsman said.

Heishiro conceded very reluctantly. While he was about to leave the hall, some of the people saw the cat eating Seishichi's rat under the veranda. On closer examination they saw that the rat was made from dried bonito (katsuo-bushi).

When this was known by the people, they were mad. To make matters worse, it became known that Seishichi himself had set up the little trick with the cat.

"Seishichi is a coward to set up such a stunt," most of the people agreed, but there were some who praised Seishichi's cunning wit.

"Well, we must give credit to Seishichi for his crafty act." The people withheld any decision on the relative merits of the two "masterpieces," so says an old tale in Osaka.

The indomitable deities

In the days of the Tokugawa Shogunate, when the country was enjoying peace and prosperity, the feudal lords used to indulge in various pastimes among themselves. One of them was wrestling.

Most of the lords had their own wrestlers, who were put into the arena to challenge the wrestlers of other lords. Naturally, the large and rich lords had stronger wrestlers. This recreation among the feudal lords, who formed the upper class of society in those days, became very popular in the middle of the Edo Period (1603-1868 A.D.).

The fief of Sasayama in the Province of Tamba was a medium-sized one. The lord at that time was called Aoyama Tadayasu. He was an ambitious and enterprising man. He served as a member of the Shogun's Council of Elders at one time, a post that not many could attain in their lifetime.

71

In those days, the wrestling tournament was held every year in the presence of the Shogun. Therefore, to have strong wrestlers was a great honor for the feudal lords. Somehow, Lord Tadayasu's wrestlers were always weak and were always eliminated in the initial round.

One year while Lord Tadayasu was brooding over the annual wrestling matches in his residence in Edo (Tokyo), he was suddenly informed of the arrival of a team of wrestlers from his fief of Sasayama.

"My Lord, ten wrestlers have just arrived from the country. They earnestly wish to be received in audience," the steward announced. Lord Tadayasu could not remember having sent any request for a wrestling team from the country. "That is strange," he thought, "I was just wondering what I should do with my weak wrestlers this year. Since they have come all the way from Sasayama, I might as well see them."

And so the wrestlers were presented to the lord. On seeing the rustic wrestlers, Lord Tadayasu felt a bit uncertain, as most of them were not as big as he had expected. Still, they looked dauntless and as if they had iron nerves, so he thought they at least possessed a fair chance of advancing into the second round.

"Steward, give these wrestlers the best treatment you can think of with the finest food and drink," Lord Tadayasu, who was known as a man of understanding, ordered.

"If, by any chance, my wrestlers can show some sign of improvement this year before the Shogun, I'll have a better chance of talking with him," Lord Tadayasu thought. He then offered prayers to all the gods in his fief, especially those of the Inari shrines (god of harvests), which were erected throughout his domain.

When the day of the wrestling tournament came, Lord Tadayasu was in an unusually good mood. He hoped for good results from his new wrestlers, and took the seat nearest the arena and the Shogun. As he had expected, all his wrestlers easily won in the first round. This feat alone was good enough to make him proud in the immediate presence of the mighty Shogun.

As the tournament progressed, contrary to the forecast and very much to the surprise of all present, the wrestlers from Sasayama finally emerged as the victors of the day.

Lord Tadayasu was elated. As soon as he returned to his residence, he ordered his steward to invite the wrestlers for a grand party to show his appreciation for their extraordinary performances.

"My Lord," the steward said somewhat perplexed, "our wrestlers have already gone. They left Edo immediately after the tournament and are on their way back to Sasayama."

"What did you say? They have already gone? They can't be far away. Call them back!"

The steward dispatched his men to call them back. The first stop for travelers in those days going down the Tokaido highway was Shinagawa. When the men came to Shinagawa, they could not find any trace of the wrestlers having stopped there. Then they searched the next stop at Hodogaya, then Odawara, Hakone, and all the possible places along the Tokaido highway, but all their efforts were in vain. Finally they reached Sasayama.

When the Karo, who was in charge of the feudal affairs in the absence of the lord, was consulted, he knew nothing of sending a team of wrestlers to Edo.

"What are the names of the wrestlers? We might be able to recognize them by their names," the Karo said.

"They are Hatonoyama, Ohchizan, Tobinoyama, Zohchizan, Shinodayama. . ."

"Hey, they certainly sound like wrestlers' names, but at the same time they are names of some of our Inari shrines. Do you think the Inari gods might have gone to Edo to help our Lord out?" one of the more learned among the retainers spoke out.

When Lord Tadayasu heard about these Inari gods, he was greatly pleased, and donated a large sum of money and other offerings to their shrines. They were thereafter known as "indomitable deities," because they had refused to be defeated in the annual wrestling tournament before the Shogun , and had upheld the honor of Sasayama.

Even today many of the Inari shrines in the city of Sasayama, Hyogo Prefecture, retain wrestlers' names that have survived through many generations.

The thunderbolt's promise

THE Japanese thunderbolt is an ogre-like being with several small drums strung around its body in a circle, living far above the clouds in the sky. It is most dreaded for its bad habit of taking people's navels, when it comes pealing down to earth from the rainy clouds.

In western Japan these thunderbolts had a unique observance once a year in summer, when the young unmarried of them engaged in a competition for brides. This happened one year in the Sanda region of the old Province of Tamba (adjoining Kyoto to the west).

Three conditions were used to judge the winner of the competition: first, to get the biggest navels, preferably from plump people; second, to get the largest number of navels; third to sound one's drums the loudest. The winner would receive the most beautiful bride. The competition started on a rainy day with thunder rolls from the great drum up above behind a gigantic cumulous cloud.

"What's that I see down below lying on the veranda of the Kinjoji temple?" one of the younger thunderbolts cried out, as it peered through a crack in the clouds. "If he is the bonze trying to cool himself, he's exactly what I am looking for: he is fat and naked, and his navel is sticking out from his 'fundoshi' (breechcloth). I must get him before it's too late." So saying he dashed forward, but stumbled over a crevice in the cloud. Before the thunderbolt knew what was going on, it was plummeting straight toward the earth off balance.

Meanwhile, when the peals of the thunder began to resound through the neighborhood together with a heavy rain, the housewives frantically rushed out to gather in their laundry. While those indoors hastily hung mosquito nets, the last defense against thunderbolt attack. A great commotion ensued throughout the village.

At length a crashing rumble was heard from the Kinjoji temple. "The temple must have been hit by a thunderbolt," some of the villagers cried out. "Let's go and help the bonze."

When the villagers reached the temple, it was as

quiet as usual, as if nothing had happened. "Dear Osho-san (bonze), are you all right in this thunderstorm?"

"What is the matter with you? Of course, I'm all right. I was dozing. But I did seem to hear a noise somewhere," the bonze said sleepily.

When the villagers heard the bonze, one of them uttered, "What a blessed bonze, I wish I could live like him."

As there seemed to be nothing wrong with the temple, the villagers began to go home. But one of them grew suspicious about the old well not far away. He went and looked into it.

"Hey! Fellows! I see a thunderbolt struggling down there," he cried out.

Sure enough, when they peeped into the well, there was a young thunderbolt crawling and floundering in agony at the bottom. Then it again called for help.

"O my dear Bonze, the most faithful servant of the Great Buddha, please have mercy on me and let me out of this well. Oh, oh, please!"

Although the bonze felt sorry for the thunderbolt, he was unwilling to release it, because the thunderbolts had been scaring the people of the Kuwabara village. He thought it was better to keep the estranged thunderbolt in the well as a punishment.

"No, you stay there until you can behave yourself," the bonze said adamantly.

For a time the thunderbolt was silent, but after a while it cried out again. "But, dear Bonze, have you ever thought why the rice crop in this region is so plentiful and the quality of the rice better than in other places?"

"Of course, I have. It's because the farmers here

are among the most hardworking people in the province. What has that got to do with you?" the bonze queried.

"I agree with you on that point. The people are truly hardworking. But you have forgotten a more important reason. Don't you know?" the thunderbolt left the bonze pondering for some time.

"What are you trying to tell me?" the bonze asked.

"The rice crop is good because we thunderbolts give the people plenty of water. Don't you see? Good rice is grown where there is plenty of fresh water."

The bonze thought for a moment and then said, "Yes, I think you're right ... All right, all right. If you will promise not to scare the people of this Kuwabara village with your drums, I'll let you go."

"Yes, I promise, Osho-san. Furthermore, I will tell the other thunderbolts not to come down to Kuwabara any more."

Thereafter, whenever there was a thunderstorm, it was a custom for the people of that part of the old Province of Tamba to cry out "Kuwabara, Kuwabara" as a charm to ward off thunderbolts.

A story of two brothers

THERE were two brothers, who possessed rather different characters, living in the southern part of the old Province of Harima, not far from the present city of Kobe. Their father was about the richest landlord in the district.

The elder of the two brothers, who was still in his late twenties, was a loose, easygoing man, a typical sloven but honest. While the younger brother was tight, stingy and sly.

One day their father called them to his room and said, "I am old, and cannot live forever, so I want one of you to inherit my vast riches. Here are one thousand gold pieces for each of you. Go out into the world and return after one year. I will give all my riches to the one who has made more money. Now go."

When the older brother heard his father's wish, he did not think much about the riches. But he was happy, very happy that he could spend one thousand gold pieces the way he wished without any worries. The first place he went was the village wineshop to drink as much as he could. After that he found himself walking with a number of pretty women in the midst of the pleasure quarters of a neighboring town. For the next several weeks he remained there, enjoying the happiest days of his life.

The younger brother, on the other hand, was greedy, and wanted to inherit the riches. With the one thousand gold pieces as capital, he opened a shop to sell sweetened rice dumpling. This made a hit with the people, and in no time he had made an enormous profit.

Several weeks passed and the elder brother found himself dead broke. There was nothing more he could do, and he had almost decided to jump into the sea to end his life. Just then he met a beautiful woman who offered to help him escape from his predicament. She led him to a magnificent mansion and said: "You can eat and drink as you like and have anything you want. After you have had enough, call me and I'll show you the way to go home."

The young man did not hesitate, because he had abandoned altogether any hope in this world. He decided to enjoy the life in the splendid mansion with all the luxuries, even though it was just for a short time. When he got tired of the plentiful life in the mansion, he asked the beautiful woman to let him go home, as he began to feel homesick.

"Good, my dear man, that is the best thing you have ever thought. As a souvenir, here is a magic bottle. It will bring you happiness. If you want anything, just ask the bottle, and it will answer you, if you turn it upside down."

The young man did not doubt the woman. As he had no money, he thought he might try the bottle. He said, "Let there be a few pieces of gold coins," and turned the small silver bottle upside down.

As soon as the bottle was turned upside down, a few gold pieces clinked out of it, very much to his amazement. "This is indeed great!" he exclaimed, but the next moment he whispered, "But I must be careful not to use it for any evil purposes." For the first time in his life he came to realize what a fool he had been until then.

After he got enough money to travel back to his father's house, he returned triumphantly, thinking that he would make his father the happiest man in the world. However, when he reached the house, the younger brother was already there with a number of chests full of gold coins.

When the father saw his two sons, he was immensely happy and eager to hear their stories saying, "Now, that you are both back, what have you to say? Let me hear from the one who came back first."

"Dear Father, with the one thousand gold pieces as capital I went into business and made a clear profit of nearly ten thousand gold pieces. I think I am a good businessman. If you will allow me to inherit your riches, you will have no worries," the greedy son said, trying to convince the father of his keen business sense.

"What have you got to say?" the father asked the elder son.

"Dear Father, I've spent all the money you gave me and now I have returned empty-handed. But while I was roaming different parts of the country and meeting all kinds of people, I learned a lot about this world. You may not believe me, but I am an entirely new man, with more wisdom, able to tell good from the bad and ready to be of help to you. Now my wisdom is invaluable. If you want gold coins to measure your riches, here they are," he said and whispered something into the silver bottle. And before long the house was filled with glittering gold coins.

And this is the kind of story the elders of the old Province of Harima used to tell their children to emphasize the value of good sense. And to impress on them the importance of the responsibilities the first-born son had to shoulder in the old family system in this country.

Value of experience —
the world —
wisdom

The dragons of
Kita-In

THERE is an old Buddhist temple called Kita-In on
the outskirts of the historic city of Kawagoe not far
north of Tokyo. It happened a very long time ago
there at the temple. One night while the abbot of
the temple was leisurely passing his time in his
study, a damsel happened to call on him.

"My dear abbot, please do me a favor, I fervently
implore you," she entreated demurely.

When the abbot heard her, he felt slightly surprised, as it was already late. He looked up to see
who could be speaking to him so sweetly. There before him was a beautiful young lady, whom he had
not seen in the neighborhood. While he watched
her, he began to wonder whether she was a phan-
tom or not.

At length he composed himself and said in a
kindly tone, as he was always good to the people,

"My dear lady, what made you come to me so late at night? And what do you want of me?"

As if the damsel had been waiting for the abbot to speak, she immediately replied, "O my merciful abbot, I have come tonight to ask you a special favor. I would like you to stop tolling your huge bell for one hundred days, starting from tonight. I beseech you. Please, my most benevolent abbot." The damsel made her request so graciously that the abbot felt overpowered by her manners.

"Who can this charming highborn damsel be?" the old abbot wondered, watching her closely. "Hmm, stop tolling the temple bell, eh?" he said pensively.

"If you will stop the bell for that length of time, I will promise to make the pealing of the bell more sonorous. It will resound farther into the neighboring districts than it does now," the young lady said to the abbot, and bowed down on the mat several times.

The aged abbot was perplexed. He had never had such an experience before, and could not decide what to do. As he kept looking at the beautiful damsel, he began to feel pity for her. Her earnestness was real; the abbot felt that if he refused her, some unknown misfortune might come upon him.

Before the abbot knew what he was doing, he found himself nodding, very much to his surprise. "Good, I will promise to stop tolling the temple bell for one hundred days."

"Thank you very much," the damsel said sweetly and bowed deep before the abbot with folded hands, as she would do to the Great Buddha.

"Strange, very strange to lure me into this trance. She must surely be a messenger from some deity. I must see where she retires," the abbot thought and decided to follow her.

When the damsel left the abbot's study, he followed her until she went out of the front gate into the darkness beyond. After that, he watched her vague figure for some distance until she came to the large pond situated not far south of the temple, where she melted into the darkness. "How mysterious. Well, there's nothing more I can do," he muttered to himself and returned to the temple.

As soon as he was back in the temple, he gave orders to stop tolling the huge bell for one hundred days. He was afraid something might happen if he did not honor the promise made to the damsel. For the first ten days he was nervous. Twenty days passed and nothing happened. Fifty days passed and still no incident. The following days were as peaceful as at normal times.

After ninety days had passed, the abbot's anxiety began to ease. "Why was I so worried for the damsel? Perhaps, I was just eager to have our bell resound more pleasantly for our parishioners," he said to comfort himself. The ninety-ninth day finally came, and the abbot was ready to heave a big sigh of relief.

While the abbot was resting in his study after supper, a young lady quite suddenly appeared before him. He was taken aback again. She was not the damsel who had visited him one hundred days ago, but she was just as beautiful.

"O my most merciful abbot . I have come to ask you one favor. Please let me hear the temple bell just once this night. I implore you with all my heart," the young lady said in the sweetest manner. Her voice strangely pierced into his heart.

After seeing how earnest this young lady was and after considerable pondering, the kindhearted abbot finally acquiesced in her wish, reflecting that nothing had happened so far for ninety-nine days and his promise to the other damsel was nearly fulfilled anyway. He ordered the priestling to peal the temple bell.

"GONG!!!"

The gong then resounded throughout the district. Before it faded, into the darkness beyond, the weather suddenly changed and in another moment a terrific rainstorm ensued. What was more wondrous, the young lady herself was transformed into a dragon and flew away into the sky, to the utter amazement of the abbot.

It was later learned that the first damsel was the spirit of a dragon living in the pond south of the temple, which abhorred the pealings of the huge temple bell. And the second young lady was the spirit of another dragon living in the nearby mountains, which was fond of the temple bell. Even today, the abbot of the Kita-In temple is very strict with the handling of the temple bell, due largely to this mysterious incident that happened a long, long time ago.

A prescription for kleptomania

A long time ago, there was a doctor called Nakarai Soju living in the city of Sakai in the old Province of Izumi (present Osaka Prefecture). He was the best doctor in the city, and his fame spread throughout the province and even to other provinces in western Japan.

"If you take medicine concocted by Soju-sensei, you can be cured of any illness in no time. He is like a god performing miracles." Everybody spoke in high praise of the doctor.

Therefore, his clinic was always crowded with people from morning till night. And he had to hire assistants to help him to tend the large number of patients coming from all over the country.

One evening an old woman came, looking sick and worried like all the other people in the waiting room. When her turn came, she was ushered before the doctor.

"Well, my dear lady. What made you come to me so late at night? Yes, you look very tired. What is the trouble with you?" Soju-sensei received her kindly.

"Dear Sensei, I'm not sick... err, I am sick in a way, but the trouble is with my son," the old woman said somewhat hesitantly.

"I see. Then what is the matter with your son?" the doctor asked.

"Sensei, he's got a bad habit, and I thought you might be able to cure him of it with your miraculous medicine," the old woman said with some embarrassment.

"A bad habit? What sort of habit? Can you tell me exactly what it is?"

The old woman cast her eyes down for a moment hesitating, then she whispered so that nobody but the doctor could hear her.

"Sensei, I'm ashamed to say it, but my son likes to steal other people's things. He is a habitual thief. What's worse, he is getting cleverer and bolder, and I'm afraid in time he may become a notorious outlaw like Ishikawa Goemon. Oh, oh, Sensei, please help him to return to his normal, honest self," the old woman pleaded earnestly.

So far Soju-sensei had heard many sad tales. But this was the first of its kind he had listened to, so he was somewhat uncertained how to treat the worried woman. But he could not stay silent, so he replied in an assured manner.

"Oh, that's too bad, my dear lady. It's an exceptional case, but I'll prescribe something very good for your son. Don't worry, don't worry," he said and even patted the old woman's back to soothe her, while taking her back to the waiting room.

"Thank you, Sensei. If you can cure his bad habit, it's the only wish I have in my life. And I can die without any worries," the old woman said; bowing ever so reverently, as if worshipping the doctor.

The doctor disappeared into his workroom, made the medicine and brought it to the old woman saying, "Now, here is a special medicine prescribed by me for your son. It's in powder form. Tell him to take one pack every time he has the urge to steal. The best time is just as he starts to act. That is important."

"Thank you, Sensei. I will tell my son exactly what you have told me. I thank you many, many times again," the old woman said with the utmost gratitude and went home.

As soon as the old woman left the doctor's office, the doctor's assistants, who had been watching these proceedings, looked at each other doubtfully. Then one of them whispered, "I know our Master is the best in the country, but I've never seen anything like today's case before. It may be a new disease of the nervous system. Let's go and ask him about it."

When the doctor was consulted by his assistants about the new prescription to cure habitual thievery, he said, "The new medicine I gave the old woman will surely cure her son's bad habit. This would be a good problem for you to try your wits on. If you cannot solve it, come to me in a day or two."

There were several assistants, and they wracked their brains for two days and two nights. But as they could not come to any satisfactory solution, they went back to their master.

"Sensei, we've discussed the problem of your anti-theft prescription for two days, but we cannot find the solution of it. Will you please tell us what new drug you have used for this new sickness?" the assistants approached their master.

"Well, fellows, you haven't used your heads enough. It's not a new ailment of the nerves. Indeed, most robbers and thieves have strong nerves. It's more a predilection that one possesses innately that draws them into bad habits. When the old woman told me about her son's stealing habit, I immediately thought of interrupting the act. So, I prescribed a new powder medicine which will dry the lung. When one's lung is dry, he coughs. How can you steal anything when you start to cough? You'll be heard and get caught. Don't you see?"

Jubei's eyeglasses

THERE was an old woodcutter called Jubei. He lived all alone in a mountainous village in the western end of the Province of Tosa. He was so tight that he was known among his friends as "Stingy Jubei."

One day the old woman, who lived next door, came to Jubei and said, "My dear Jubei, alas, you have come to this age without taking a wife. While you were young and healthy, life was easy, but now at sixty, things must be hard on you. If you have anything to wash I'll do it for you, poor man."

"Thank you, thank you, but I'm used to doing for myself from my younger days, and I've never felt any inconvenience. Besides, if I ask anyone to wash things for me, I'll have to pay, you know."

"That's why you need a wife. You wouldn't have to pay her anything, you know what I mean," she said, trying to convince him.

"Yes, I know exactly what you mean, but if I take a

wife, I'll have to feed her. That's what I don't want to do," Jubei said, lightly rejecting the woman's advice.

One day in autumn while he was working in the mountains, he started to sharpen the teeth of his large saw with a file, as they were a bit dull. Due to his age and out of necessity he had to use eyeglasses, which he had bought only recently but very reluctantly after many weeks of brooding.

At length he felt thirsty, so he walked down a ravine to refresh his thirst at the stream flowing there. When he came back he saw a monkey with his valuable eyeglasses on. The monkey was meddling noisily with the saw file, imitating what he had been doing. He was astonished, and shouted furiously to frighten the monkey away, "Hey, you darn fool! What have you been doing?" Then he began to chase the monkey away.

The monkey, taken by surprise, jumped up several feet into the air and disappeared in the bushes beyond, clutching Jubei's eyeglasses. Jubei was mad with rage, because he could not work on the saw without the eyeglasses. That night he could not go to sleep, thinking how he might catch the monkey and get back his indispensable eyeglasses.

When he woke up the following morning, he called on one of his friends to borrow his rifle. He was determined to kill the monkey and get back his eyeglasses. Then he went into the mountains very early and after much study he took up a strategic position under a tree. It was where he could see the monkey without being noticed.

Jubei was serious and kept a close watch around him, as the monkey was also a cunning animal. However, nothing happened for a long time, and in the meantime he began to feel hungry.

"No, I'm not going to eat until I get that monkey. Besides, I haven't done anything today, so I'm not entitled to a meal," he muttered to himself to ease his anxiety.

It must have been a very long time after his usual lunch time when he began to feel thirsty. He laid the rifle erect against the tree and quietly went down the ravine toward the stream. When he reached the stream and was about to kneel down for a drink, all of a sudden there was a rifle shot BANG! which pierced the silence of the mountain.

Jubei was astounded. He quickly turned around and scrambled up the sloping path toward the tree, where he had left the rifle. When he reached there, he saw a big monkey shot through its head, bleeding to death, and a smaller monkey lying dead nearby.

While Jubei was looking at the pitiful scene, he could surmise that the big monkey must have been shot to death while looking into the nozzle of the rifle when the smaller monkey pulled the trigger. The smaller monkey must have been struck to death by the butt end of the rifle that kicked back when the rifle went off.

Although Jubei had eagerly wanted to take revenge on the big monkey for stealing his eyeglasses, he felt sorry after seeing the two monkeys dead, and carried them back to the village to show them to his friend, who had lent him the rifle.

When his friend heard Jubei's story, he said, "Why, Jubei, you always complain about losing things, but today you got two monkeys with one shot. That's a trick not everybody can do. Only the most able hunters can do such a stunt, and only rarely, you know. Why aren't you happy about it?"

"I know, I know," Jubei said sadly, "you see, the big monkey must have had my eyeglasses on when it was shot to death. And my eyeglasses were shattered to pieces. Only the metal frame was left there."

A beggar's life

O<small>NCE</small> upon a time there was a rich man known by the local people as "Choja." He lived in the eastern part of the Province of Tosa in Shikoku.

In this part of the country, the honorific "Choja" was given to a wealthy man who could provide one thousand umbrellas at any time, should a crowd of strangers happen to come running into his house on a rainy day, or anyone who could supply meals to one thousand unexpected guests.

Now, there was a young beggar always loitering under the porch of the Choja's mansion, living on the leftovers from his kitchen.

One night the beggar saw three stalwart bandits sneaking into the Choja's mansion. He was startled, but thought that if he informed the master about the bandits it would be a good chance for him to ask for employment. But he thought again and realized that if he got caught by the bandits he would be killed. "No, it's too risky, it would not pay," he reconsidered and decided to keep watch over the bandits.

A few minutes later, he saw the three bandits coming out of the mansion, each carrying a small chest containing one thousand gold coins. The beggar stealthily followed the three bandits for about a mile, when they came to a river. They then sank the heavy chests in the middle of the river under one of the girders, and disappeared into the darkness.

The following morning when the beggar went to the kitchen for his breakfast, there was a great commotion in the big mansion. So he asked the maids what it was all about. He was told that three chests of gold coins had been stolen last night, and everybody in the mansion was ordered to go in search of them.

"My dear maid, I happen to be a fortuneteller. If the master is so worried I can help him, you know," the beggar said.

At first the maid paid no attention to him, but when the steward of the Choja heard about it, he consulted with his master. "Well, let's try the beggar, as it won't cost me any money," the master said and called him in.

When the beggar was brought before the master, he asked for a handful of chopsticks as divining rods. The beggar then grabbed the chopsticks and solemnly cast them on the floor before him a number of times to stir up the tension of those watching him. Then he closed his eyes and pronounced his findings in a dignified manner like a real conjurer.

"The three chests of gold coins are sunk in the middle of a river under the girder of a bridge, about a mile to the east of this mansion."

The master immediately sent his steward and sure enough the three chests were found intact.

"My dear man, I am greatly indebted to you. From today on, you will be my personal guest and stay with us in this mansion," the master said.

In this way the beggar, whose name was Sansuke, began a new life. In the meantime, his fame became so great that one day he was summoned by the Lord of the province to help him find a lost treasure.

When Sansuke got the invitation, he was frightened to death, and thought, "If the Lord finds out that I am a fake fortuneteller, I know I will be beheaded." But then he thought, "If I refuse him, I may meet the same fate. In that case, I might as well go and meet a great man like him before I die."

The following day he went to the castle, and to his surprise he was lavishly entertained with all sorts of rich foods he had never seen in his life. Toward evening, after the long entertainment, Sansuke was brought before the Lord. Being a clever man he said, "My dear Lord, in my world we usually augur in the morning, when we are in the best of condition," thinking at the same time he had prolonged his life for one more night.

Although the Lord was anxious to hear his augury, he conceded to Sansuke's wishes. When Sansuke went to bed he could not go to sleep. While he was lingering, he heard someone knocking at the door softly.

"Who are you? And what do you want of me?" Sansuke asked.

"I am one of the retainers of the Lord, and I happen to know where the lost treasure is hidden. If you will promise not to ask my name, I will tell you about it. You see, I stole the treasure, and I want to give it back." In this way Sansuke learned the location of the lost treasure.

The next morning, Sansuke told the Lord that the treasure was hidden in an old, crumbling Jizo temple some miles away from the castle, as indeed it was. After he had successfully finished his work at the castle, Sansuke vowed he would never again bluff his way with fake augury.

Many months passed, and one day the only daughter of the Choja was suddenly taken ill. Naturally, Sansuke was asked to cast his divining rods. That night while he was wondering how he could get out of this case, an apparition appeared at his bedside. "Sansuke," it said, "I am the Jizo Deity of the dilapidated temple, which the Lord has rebuilt handsomely. As a token of my thanks to you, I will tell you the cause of the daughter's illness. There is the skeleton of a white mouse buried under her room."

The next day the skeleton was reburied with due respect, and the daughter gradually began to recover. In time, Sansuke was married to her for saving her life. He inherited the vast riches, but he ceased to be a fortuneteller in order to uphold the dignity of the Choja family. He changed his lowly name of Sansuke to the more dignified Sannojo, and lived happily with his wife ever afterward.

A Koshikijima tale

THE Koshikijima islands are a group of small islands scattered in the sea off the shores of Kagoshima, the southernmost part of Kyushu. These islands have many unique folktales.

Once upon a time there was a man called Chubei living with his beautiful wife. But he was so poor that he could not even pay the small tax due yearly. One day he said to his wife, "I have finally decided to go to work somewhere to make money for our taxes. But will you please stay in this house until I come back?"

The wife felt a bit sorry, but she agreed to stay until he came back.

Chubei went to Osaka and fortunately found a job with a rich man, who promised to pay him well. Being robust, he withstood even the roughest labor. At the end of one year, he had made more money than he had expected. Therefore, he decided to go back to the island before his beautiful wife was taken away by some other man.

When he left Osaka, he had with him thirty gold coins, which was more than enough to pay his taxes. As he was in great hurry, he walked day and night to be nearer his wife. One night it became so dark that he could not see where he was walking, but he perceived a small speck of light in the far distance. On reaching the light he found a shack, and inside he saw an old man.

"Pardon," he said and asked for a night's rest.

Then the old man said, "Are you fond of stories? If you are not, I cannot accommodate you," and looked at him for an immediate answer.

Chubei did not know how to answer. He thought that if he said "no," there would not be a chance in the world of finding another place for the night, so he reluctantly acceded. And he was permitted to spend the night there. When he sat down by the fireplace, the old man said, "Well, my dear man, my story will cost you quite a bit. Are you ready? "

"Yes, if it is not too much," Chubei said, but had a premonition that the old man's story would be expensive. "Good. Now, listen. On a rainy night, avoid any rocky shelter. The price is ten gold coins."

"Darn you," Chubei thought and wanted to curse him more, but since it was a gentlemen's agreement, he had to obey, and paid him ten gold coins.

The next morning Chubei hurriedly left the shack. Toward evening the weather suddenly changed, and a heavy rainstorm ensued. Chubei ran in the rainstorm for some time until he came to the foot of a rocky hill, where he found a cave.

"What luck," he said and jumped into the cave, but the next moment he recalled how he had lost the ten gold pieces, so he jumped out of the cave. No sooner had he left the cave than he heard a great noise. He looked back and saw the whole hill crumble away in the rain.

The following night Chubei again lost his way and after wandering he found a shack where there was an old man, just like the night before. He asked for a night's rest.

"Young man, you may stay here, but you must listen to my story, which will cost you a lot. Can you pay?"

"I will pay rather than go out into the darkness," he answered without hesitating.

"Good. Now, the longest way around is the shortest way home. Ten gold coins for that."

Chubei paid him the ten gold coins. The next day he came to a ferry. Just as he was about to step on board the ferryboat, he recalled how he had lost ten gold pieces the night before, so he decided to take the longer way by land. While he was walking, he saw the overloaded ferryboat sink, and all the passengers were washed away downstream.

After some days Chubei lost his way again at night, but fortunately he met an old man, who took him to his house. "My dear man, you must pay dearly for one night's lodging in this house."

"Yes, how can that be?" Chubei asked.

"Haste makes waste. The price is ten gold coins."

In this way Chubei lost all his money. He did not know what to do. But as his house was near, he finally decided to go back and see how things had progressed in the meantime.

When he reached his house, it was night. Fortunately nobody had seen him. So he peeped into his own house from a crack. There he saw his wife serving sake (rice wine) to the priest of a nearby Buddhist temple. He was astounded, and hot with jealousy. He was about to rush into the house, when he recalled the words "haste makes waste," which had cost him his last ten gold coins. After a while he

regained his usual composure, and knocked the door. "Hi, my dear, I'm back from Osaka," he said and waited for a time for the priest to hide.

When the priest heard the husband's call, he jumped into a vat and hid himself.

When Chubei went inside, he found the table ready for a sake party. "You see, I had a dream last night that you would be back soon, so I have been waiting for your return," the wife said and welcomed her husband affectionately.

Chubei pretended he had not seen anything, so he looked around and when he saw the vat, he asked what it was for.

"Oh, that? I made some 'miso (bean paste)' for the temple," she said rather calmly.

"So," Chubei said admiring her wit. "Fine, but it's too heavy for you; I'll take it to the temple," he said and carrying it on his back he brought it to the temple.

At the temple a priestling came out, so Chubei said, "Hey, young man, this is the 'miso' my wife made for this temple. I want five hundred gold coins for it. While I use your toilet outside, you get ready with the money."

When Chubei went outside, the priest came out of the vat and ordered the priestling, "Get out five hundred gold coins from my drawer for him."

In this way the man got five hundred gold coins, and he lived happily with his beautiful wife ever afterward.

The adventure of Gembei the hunter

ONCE upon a time there was a wise hunter called Gembei living in the central mountains of the Province of Hyuga. One day he went hunting as usual into the nearby hills, shouldering his favorite rifle with which he had never missed a shot in his life. That day, unfortunately, he found no game in the forenoon, so in the afternoon he went deeper into the mountains.

While he was anxiously trekking along the narrow path, a little hare suddenly appeared in front of him, prancing a few feet to the right and then to the left, without giving him time to set his rifle. This continued for some time, when a huge monster suddenly leaped on the poor hare from a clump of bushes.

At first Gembei was startled at this unexpected appearance, and when he saw what it was he was even more startled. It was a giant serpent. Instead of swallowing the hare, the serpent kept it hanging between its teeth, as if to tease the hunter.

"Darn you! I'll get you for this!" Gembei cried out, aiming his rifle at the serpent. When the serpent saw Gembei leveling the rifle, it quickly retreated and disappeared into the thicket beyond.

Gembei followed the trail left by the serpent and went deeper and deeper into the mountains. After hours of pursuit, he finally spotted the serpent, which had climbed up into a huge pine tree, and was about to swallow the poor hare.

"No, sir. That hare is mine," Gembei said and aiming his rifle at the serpent's head, he pulled the trigger. "BANG!"

Sure enough Gembei's shot hit the serpent's head, and the hare fell down to the ground. Then the serpent's long body, which was wound around the tree seven times, began to writhe furiously in agony. Gembei waited until the serpent had finally expired, then he went over to pick up the hare and hurriedly left the bloody spot.

As he was so deep in the mountains, he knew he could not get out before sunset. He decided to pass the night in the woods, and began to build a fire under a large tree. While he was grilling the hare

郵便はがき

料金受取人払

小石川局承認

1081

差出有効期間
平成6年4月
16日まで

1 1 2 -

東京都文京区音羽
一丁目十七番十四号

講談社インターナショナル
愛読者カード係

お名前 NAME		
年 齢 AGE	□ 女性 FEMALE □ 男性 MALE	
ご住所・郵便番号 ADDRESS		
お仕事 OCCUPATION	国 籍 NATIONALITY	

本書の内容、装幀などについてご意見をお聞かせ下さい。
Impression of this book (content, design, etc.)

Our aim is to promote cultural exchange between East and West. We are interested in your suggestions. 今後の出版企画の参考にいたしたく存じます。ご記入の上、ご投函下さいますようお願いいたします。

1. Title of book： ＿＿＿＿＿＿＿＿＿＿＿＿＿＿＿＿＿
   書名

2. Where did you purchase this book?
   本書をどこでお求めになりましたか？

   □ at a bookstore   (name   )
   　 書店にて   　書店名

   □ elsewhere   (name   )
   　 その他の場所で

   □ a gift
   　 プレゼント

3. How did you hear about this book?
   本書をどこでお知りになりましたか。

   □ at a bookstore　書店にて

   □ in an advertisement　広告で (name   )
   　 新聞・雑誌名

   □ in a book review　書評・記事で (name   )
   　 新聞・雑誌名

   □ other　その他   (   )

4. Suggestions for future books (author, subject matter, etc.)
   今後出版を希望される企画、作品、作家などをお聞かせ下さい。

for his supper, he began to hear rustling noises gradually coming nearer and nearer. "Anything could happen in this darkness," he thought, and steeled himself for an emergency. Just as he was about to face the noises, a deep voice reverberated over him, "Give me that fragrant meat! If you don't, I'll kill you!"

Gembei felt terrified and trembled all over, but he forced himself to turn around to see who it was. What he saw was a huge mouth wide open not far away. It was a giant toad.

"You must wait a few minutes more, this is still raw!" Gembei quickly responded to gain time. And then he took his large hatchet out from his pouch and put it into the burning fire.

The fire was strong, so it quickly burned out the wooden handle, leaving only the iron part, which was soon red hot. When Gembei saw that it was ready, he cried out, "Now, open your mouth wide, here comes the grilled meat!" and flung the red hot iron into the toad's mouth.

"YOUCH! ! !"

The giant toad was completely taken off guard. It trampled the bushes in agony and disappeared into the darkness. Gembei felt relieved when no more noise was heard from the direction in which the toad had retreated.

After finishing his supper of the long-awaited grilled hare, Gembei started to clear the ground beside the fire to lie down to rest. But as he was about to sit down, he heard heavy footsteps coming from the darkness, and in another minute someone called out loudly, "Hey, stranger, are you going to stay here tonight?"

The man who emerged from the darkness was a hunter carrying a rifle, who appeared friendly and harmless, but there was something sinister about him that caught Gembei's keen eye. "Yes, I am," he replied, without even looking up to see him.

"Well, have a good rest," the hunter said with a smile and departed.

After the hunter had gone away, Gembei lay down to sleep, but he felt a premonition. So he stood up again and made a dummy of himself lying by the fireside. Then he hid himself in the nearby bush to watch what might happen.

Gembei waited for a very long time. As he had expected, there finally came a faint rustling noise from the direction in which the hunter had gone earlier in the evening. The noise came nearer, then stopped, and after a short pause, a rifle shot suddenly broke the silence, "BANG!"

"I guess I got him square in the head," someone whispered not far away.

A few seconds later a human figure appeared near Gembei's dummy. Gembei shot his rifle at it "BANG!" The figure tumbled over the dummy, making a light thud followed by a deep groan then it ran away into the darkness.

The following morning Gembei traced the blood-stains on the ground and finally came to a large cave. At the entrance to the cave he found the hunter he had met the night before. He had bled to death. Gembei found a whole pile of gold coins, precious jewels, and other treasures in the cave, all undoubtedly· stolen from innocent people. Although he reported his find to the local magistrate, it was given to him, because the magistrate did not want to be involved with stolen goods.

Gembei spent the rest of his life in peace and ease.

The Kappa's ointment

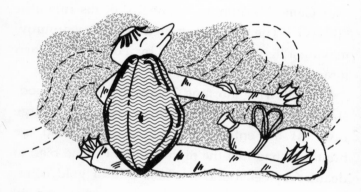

A long time ago there was a strong man called Jutaro living in the village of Futago near the Kita-kamigawa (river), which flowed through the western part of the Province of Rikuzen.

As the village was near the river, the villagers were often molested by a mischievous kappa (water imp) living there. It used to pick on the womenfolk and children, coming almost nightly into the village to harm them, especially when they were in the bath or toilet.

Jutaro the strong man heard stories of the kappa's mischief, and decided to see for himself whether they were true or not. He happened to be very skilful in swordsmanship, and so one night he disguised himself as a woman, with a maiden's coiffure. He went into the bathhouse to bathe. While he was washing, he felt something behind him. He turned around to see what it was, and to his surprise he saw a big, sinewy arm, extending from the small opening.

Jutaro was horror-stricken, but as he had been expecting something to happen, he was prepared. He quickly unsheathed his sword and struck the hideous arm as hard as he could. The blow must have been terrific. The arm was severed and fell into the bathtub. There was silence outside. Jutaro then heard someone running away.

The next morning Jutaro brought the severed arm to the village Buddhist temple. "My dear abbot, last night...," and then he related the whole story.

"I see. This is unmistakably the arm of a kappa, and it must be that of the rascal doing harm to the womenfolk and children these days. It has been said from olden times that these abominable beings always come back to reclaim what they have lost within seven days. So you must be on guard, my dear man, or you'll surely lose your own life," the kindly priest advised.

Jutaro then asked the priest to impound the arm in a box with the almighty power of the Great Buddha, so that the kappa could not come to reclaim it. Five days passed and nothing happened in the meantime, but Jutaro could not stop worrying. There were two days left for the kappa to lay claim to his arm.

On the night of the sixth day, Jutaro saw an apparition at his bedside. Drawing himself up to his full height, he addressed the ghost in the dim light fearlessly: "Who are you standing there?"

"I have come not to harm you. I am here to apologize for the many wrongs done to your womenfolk and children. Will you please return me the arm? Please, I beg you."

When Jutaro heard these pleading words, he drew his sword nearer to him, and cried out, "So, you are the rascal who has been molesting our good people. If I catch you the next time, I'll cut your head off. Get away from here as quickly as you can, or I'll really use my sword."

But the apparition would not move. It prostrated itself on the floor, against which it pressed its head as if repenting deeply, and whispered very contritely,

"I understand how hateful I am. I am the kappa living down in the river. Please forgive me for all my wrongdoings of the past."

Seeing this pitiful sight Jutaro began to feel a bit sorry. At length he lowered his posture and said, "Are you sure you will never harm the womenfolk and children again? If so, I may forgive you. But I cannot return your arm. It is firmly inclosed in a box sealed with the almighty power of the Great Buddha. I'll spare your life this time, but get away from here and never come back to the village again."

When the kappa heard him, it gave out a deep sigh and said, "If you'll forgive me, really pardon my wrongdoings, that's what I need. Then I can reclaim my arm wherever it is stored. It is mine, after all. I can have it back in no time."

"What did you say? You can get it back anytime from anywhere, even from the box sealed with the Great Buddha's blessings?"

"Yes, certainly," and the kappa began to chant a weird incantation. In another moment his severed arm was before him.

Jutaro was astonished to see such magic. "If you can so easily get it back, why come all the way to me to play your trick on me?"

"As I have said before, I must first get your permission. Unless I get the owner's assent, my power will not work. Now, if you want anything for giving me back my arm, I shall be glad to grant your wish."

"Well, but what are you going to do with your severed arm?"

"This?" the kappa said holding up his severed arm, "I can put it back where it belongs with this ointment."

"Try it, and let me see how it works."

The kappa then smeared a bit of the ointment on its elbow, from where the arm had been severed, and placed the arm there. In a moment the arm was stuck firmly in place, and it began to move as before.

"Miraculous!" Jutaro cried out, "let me see whether I can see the wound." There was no trace of anything there. "Would it work on human beings too?" he asked.

"Yes, I'll give you some, and I'll show you how to prepare it, too, though it's one of the most valuable secrets of us kappas."

Thereafter, as has been told and retold in that part of the northern province Jutaro prospered for many generations as the originator of this miracle ointment that healed wounds and injuries of all kinds.

Jinnai's dreamland

JINNAI was one of those happy-go-lucky men, living in a quiet mountainous village in the central part of the northern Province of Rikuchu. However, he was very fond of his family. He always thought of his wife and children whenever he went on a journey. And he hurried home as soon as his errands were done.

One day early in the morning he went out of the house to take in the refreshing air, when he perceived something like a human being standing on the top of a hill not far away. On closer look, he could faintly make out somebody beckoning to him in the early morning mist. He had no idea why he should be called by anyone. So he did not even try to confirm whether the faint figure was really beckoning to him, and stepped back into the house.

The following morning he woke up early and, as he had the day before, went out of the house to take in the refreshing air. Then he looked up toward the hill and there he clearly saw a young woman standing, waving her hands to catch his attention. When Jinnai's eyes met hers, she beckoned to him to come up the hill.

"Who can she be? I don't recognize her. I swear she has never been in this part of the country before. How strange," Jinnai began to wonder.

He had no intention of answering her, thinking she must be mistaking him for someone else, so without much thought he went back into his house. He did not even mention her to his wife, nor to anyone else in the family.

The next morning when Jinnai went out of the house, although the morning mist was still floating around, he could see the same young woman standing at the top of the hill. This time she urgently beckoned him to come up the slope. The thought struck Jinnai that it might be fun to meet her, and ask her what she wanted him for.

As Jinnai walked up the slope and finally reached her, he could see her beautiful face beaming with happiness.

"Ah, my dearest Jinnai. I have your promise to make me your wife, so I've been waiting for you here every morning. Now, please come to my house," the young lady said with the most lovable voice Jinnai had ever heard. She immediately took his hand to lure him away.

Jinnai was stunned. He could not remember ever meeting her, or making any promise of any kind to such a lovely lady. But before he could realize what was happening the young lady was tightly hugging his arm and leading him down the other side of the hill.

When they reached the foot of the hill, and stepped over a bunker, he thought he felt something strange around him. The scenery suddenly changed to a wonderful world; the stream was limpid with crystalline water that sparkled like jewels, the verdant trees glistened all over in a greenish hue, and the fields were studded with all kinds of colorful flowers, and even the birds made fascinating music, making Jinnai feel as if he were in perfect bliss in heaven.

Before long Jinnai and the lovely lady came upon a gorgeous mansion, from where a bevy of pretty maids rushed out to welcome them. Jinnai by this time had become used to the new surroundings. He began to enjoy the dreamlike life.

"So, this is what they call 'heavenly life,'" he said to himself, after spending a few rosy days and forgetting all about his family.

It must have been about a month when he began to recall his sudden escapade with the lovely lady and the worries he might be causing his family and the villagers. But he had no heart to tell this to the lady.

"Please do not worry about your family. Your wife and the children are well taken care of by us. All you need to do is to make me happy in this mansion," the lovely lady said.

As for Jinnai himself, he began to love the lady more, and had no intention of parting with her.

"But I cannot love you thinking about my wife and family at the same time. If you will let me go back once and see how well they are faring, then I will come back and spend the rest of my life with you," Jinnai one day confided.

"If you are so anxious, you may go. But remember, if you tell anything about us to anyone, we will not be able to resume our blissful life again. Please pledge you will keep our secret," the lady said to Jinnai.

"Yes, I promise," he said and started on his way back to his house beyond the hill.

When he reached home, he found his wife, children, all his relations, friends and the priest of the village Buddhist temple holding a memorial service.

"Why Jinnai, where have you been? This is the third anniversary service of your sudden disappearance," the priest said, welcoming him at the same time.

So Jinnai had to make up all kinds of stories about how he had roamed throughout the country, visiting the Grand Shrine at Ise, then Kyoto, Osaka and other places. All the people were well satisfied, and the sad memorial service changed into a lively party.

That night, when everybody had gone away, and Jinnai was in bed with his wife, she turned to him and said, "I know you have lied. Now, tell me exactly who is the woman."

She pressed him so hard that finally he had to tell her all about the lovely lady. As soon as he had finished his story, a terrific bolt of lightning pierced Jinnai's bed room, making him an invalid for the rest of his life.

And this is one of the favorite tales told by the womenfolk in that part of the northern province.

The three horsemen

IT was a long, long time ago.

One year in early spring three young villagers in the northern Province of Rikuzen went on a pilgrimage to the Grand Shrine of Ise. They went there to pray for a bountiful year, like many other people of the country.

After many days of journeying they came to a little town and took lodging at an inn for travelers of their kind.

"Welcome, welcome, young men. Young as you are, how admirable of you to make a pilgrimage to the Ise Shrine. For your most pious devotion we will offer you the most comfortable room with the richest dishes to commemorate your auspicious journey," the master of the inn most courteously received the three young villagers.

The three men were surprised to be welcomed so hospitably in such a strange place, so the eldest of them hurriedly said, "My dear Master, we are just plain farmers with healthy appetites. As we are just doing the same thing as other people, please do not bother to entertain us so lavishly."

"Don't mind, don't mind. It has been our custom to treat everybody kindly, particularly those devoted people going to the Ise Shrine."

At length a gorgeous meal was served, and among the dishes there was a big plate full of mugwort rice cakes, one of the famed delicacies of the district. The young men, true to their healthy appetites, devoured everything placed before them, especially the rare mugwort rice cakes.

Well satisfied with the exceptional treatment, the young men went to bed and slept soundly until the next morning. When they woke up, they began to feel uneasy all over their bodies, and before they could identify the feeling, they began to see themselves changing into horses. Before long they found themselves completely changed into handsome farm horses, ready to be sold for handsome prices.

"What is this all about? Am I dreaming?" the eldest of them thought and tried to call for help, but all he could hear was the neighing of a horse. And then he looked around to see what had happened to his companions; one was being led to the nearby stable by the master of the inn, and the other was neighing roughly, shaking its head up and down furiously.

"What a life we must lead from now on," he sighed sorrowfully in great despair, imagining the miserable time all farming horses must endure throughout their lives.

While he was forlornly abandoning all hope of returning to his former self, thinking how happy he had been with his family, he quite suddenly happened to recall an old story told by his grandmother: while he was still a child that if one ate the striped pampas grass grown in the deep mountains he would be changed back into a human being.

"Now, what was the name of the place? It was not far, if my memory is correct. But anyway, this is no place for me. I must get away from here before I get thrown into the stable," he said and began to trot and then galloped away as fast as he could.

While he was running away, he tried to recall the mountain or the valley where the rare striped pampas grass grew.

"Yes, yes. I've got it. There was a swamp, around which the striped pampas grass grew, and it's in the far recess of the Nasunogahara. Hurrah!!" he cried out, but it only sounded like a loud neigh of an ordinary horse.

In time he reached the marsh and to his great surprise he saw a whole field of striped pampas grass. However, he was so tired that all he could do was eat as much pampas grass as possible, and collapsed inertly by the marshside.

When he came to again, he was no longer a four-legged horse, but a strong young man.

"This is miraculous! Almighty Buddha, thank you, thank you. But I cannot linger here any longer, as I must rescue the other two men. I will thank you more after I get them back into their kimonos. So, excuse me for the moment," he said and hurried back to the inn, with an armful of striped pampas grass.

It was already night, when he reached the inn. So he stealthily walked over to the stable, where the other two men-turned-horses were, and let them eat all the striped pampas grass he brought with him.

Early the next morning three young men walked out of the stable, but before they left there they sneaked into the kitchen and stole a plateful of mugwort rice cakes. And then they continued on their pilgrimage to the Grand Shrine at Ise.

After the pilgrimage the three men stopped at a sweet shop. They asked the shopkeeper to make a new-kind of sweet, mixing the mugwort rice cake with the conventional one of the shop. When the new sweets were made, the three men returned to the inn. They disguised themselves so that they would not be recognized, and gave the new sweets to the inn keeper as their token of thanks.

"Ah, thank you, thank you. How thoughtful of you to remember us. Yes, yes, let me taste it...," he praised the sweets and gave some to his faithful servants.

The next morning the three young men stayed at the inn just long enough to see a number of husky working horses running amok in the backyard of the inn. Then they started to walk back triumphantly toward home, as if they had conquered the whole world.

The celestial nymph

ONCE upon a time there was a timid young farmer called Jinta living in a mountainous village in the northern Province of Rikuchu. He was so shy that he avoided the other villagers, and spent his days for the most part on his small farm.

One day he went fishing in a pond far up in the mountains, which the villagers only rarely visited. While he was enjoying the serene solitude of the mountain pond, he happened to notice something glittering on a large rock that protruded into the pond not far away.

Out of curiosity he walked over to see what it was. When he came near the big rock, he heard something splashing beyond it, so he stealthily peeked over it to see what it was.

"Ah, a nymph," he whispered. "This must be her celestial robe," he said quietly to himself upon seeing a white, shining cloth lying before him. "This is

going to be a treasure for me," he thought and decided to take it to his hut.

When he reached his hut, he took out the robe and
began to admire it. It looked so lovely and precious
that at first he felt stunned to think that he could own
such a valuable piece of clothing. While still admiring it, he suddenly thought of wearing it to see
whether he could fly to the heavens like the nymph.
He then put it on and jumped from a high spot several times, but the best he could do was to land on
his bottom each time.

"No, this is of no use to me. What shall I do now?"

As he was wondering what to do with the robe, someone knocked at his door.

"Hey, Jinta, what are you making so much noise for in your hut?" someone called from the outside.

Jinta was taken aback. He quickly pushed the robe into the cupboard and went to the door to answer the call.

"Ah, welcome, Gombei… ah… Welcome… yes, what can I do for you?" said Jinta, who was upset and did not know what to do.

Gombei was by trade a horse trader, but he was known more as a viperous rogue. And so as soon as he entered the hut he looked around and did not fail to see the sleeve of the robe sticking out from the cupboard.

"Now, Jinta, don't you try to hide anything from me. Be honest. When are you going to get married?" said Gombei, thinking he was hiding a wedding dress.

And so Jinta had to confess, and told him all about the celestial robe.

"If you can't fly in it, it won't be of any use to me. No, before I incur the wrath of the celestial people, let me get away from here," Gombei said and started to leave.

"Gombei, for Buddha's sake, wait. Please take it

away from me, and you can dispose of it as you wish," Jinta begged him. Gombei was a crafty man. He knew he could sell the robe at the town pawnshop some miles away, so he took it and left Jinta's hut.

Soon afterward the celestial nymph came to Jinta's hut, clad now in makeshift garb of leaves and scrubs. "My dear man, I have followed your footprints to this hut. Please give me back my robe, which you have stolen from me. Unless I have it I cannot go back to my people in heaven," she earnestly entreated.

Jinta felt sorry, but as he had no excuse to offer, he told her all about Gombei. After she had listened to Jinta's story, which she discerned to be true, she said:

"I am told that you human beings are very greedy. Your friend, Gombei, will surely go to a pawnshop and sell my robe, for which he will get a lot of money. If you will build me a shack and give me a loom, I will weave a mandala, a tapestry of the Great Buddha and all the other deities around him. Then you can sell it and with the money you can buy back my robe. I can weave the tapestry in three days if you will bring five bundles of the stems of lotus leaves every day. Now, please go and locate my robe," she urged him.

Jinta was very much relieved to think that he could

somehow get the robe back. In the meantime the crafty Gombei had tried a number of pawnshops in the neighborhood, but they were all too tight. So he went to a draper, who was willing to pay fifty gold pieces for it. He was elated. He immediately went into a wineshop to celebrate his unexpected success.

Just as Gombei came out of the wineshop he met Jinta, who told him that the nymph had come to his hut to look for the robe. However, Gombei pretended he was dead drunk and would not tell him where he had disposed of the robe. So that Jinta had to go to every pawnshop in the whole district. When he finally found the draper, Jinta was told that the robe had already been presented to the Lord of the province, who happened to be a great connoisseur.

When the nymph heard Jinta's story, she said, "Do not worry, let us present this tapestry to the Lord, and I will remain in the castle to weave more, but you must say that I am a mute."

The tapestry was finished the following day, and Jinta presented it to the Lord, who fell in love with the beautiful piece of work at first sight.

"Wonderful!" the Lord exclaimed. "If this woman can weave another, she can stay here."

"But my Lord, she is a mute, and besides she is very

irritable, so you must let her have her own ways until she becomes used to the life in the castle," Jinta advised the Lord.

In this way she was allowed to enter the castle and stay until the time came for her to work. At first she pretended to be trying to get used to her new surroundings. But she was searching for clues that might lead her to the whereabouts of her robe. Several weeks passed. And the time came for the Lord's people to air all his precious things. After they were taken out in the open compound of the castle, the nymph, who had been waiting for the chance, eagerly searched for her robe.

When she saw her long-lost robe among other rare articles, she quickly put it on and soon flew up into the sky. All the people were taken by surprise. They began to clamor and exclaim over this un-heard-of stunt by a mute girl.

It is said that the celestial nymph did not forget to fly over Jinta's hut to bid him goodbye. The tapestry, now kept at the Buddhist temple of Komyoji in that mountain village, is still believed by the people to be the one woven by the celestial nymph a long, long time ago.

The camphor tree tale

ONCE upon a time there was a young hunter living in the town of Tomie, to the north of Nagasaki. It was his yearly practice to present a boar to the lord of the province at the end of the year as a New Year's gift.

And so one wintry day he went into the mountains to look for his prey, but somehow he failed to get any. So he made several more trips into the deep mountains, but all in vain. "Tomorrow is the last day of the year, and I must get one today by all means," the hunter muttered and walked out of the house.

Just then his wife called to him from behind. "My dear, please stay at home today. I feel as if I am going to give birth..."

The hunter hesitated for a moment, and then said reluctantly, "But I must get the animal before the night watch bell tolls from the temple. Be patient, please," and he walked away.

When he came to the foothills of the nearby mountain, it began to rain, and before long the rain became so heavy that he had to seek shelter. Fortunately there was a big camphor tree not far away.

"Ah, what a luck," the hunter sighed as he reached the camphor tree. To his surprise there was a large hollow in the side of the tree that was big enough for him to take shelter.

Meanwhile, it became dark while he was waiting for the rain to stop, which was still falling heavily. While he was plotting how he might catch a boar, he heard several voices coming toward him in the heavy rain. At length they came very close to him, but he could not see anyone as it was already dark.

Then one of them said, "Hello, fellow Camphor, we are on our way to the village down there to witness a childbirth. Are you coming with us?"

"Ah, thank you, thank you. The truth is that I've been waiting for it, but I have a guest tonight. If I go, he will get wet. So I'll have to stay here. Please go without me."

The hunter was taken aback. "What is this all about? 'A childbirth in the village.' It sounds like my own affair. But I can't do anything in this downpour."

While the hunter was imagining all kinds of possibilities, the mysterious voices came back talking noisily among themselves.

"Ah, here we are back from the village, my dear fellow Camphor. The baby is a boy. But the poor child, he can only live seven years. He is destined to die on the third day of the third month of his seventh year..."

The hunter was astounded. "If that child happens to be my own son, I can't be loitering in a place like this. I must hurry home and see things for myself," he thought and ran down toward the village as fast as he could in the heavy rain.

When he reached home, drenched all over, sure enough, his wife had just given birth to a baby boy. "So, if what I've heard in the hollow of the camphor tree is true, I must do everything for this boy," he thought and from that moment onward he vowed to devote all his time to his son. However, he did not tell anyone what he had heard under the camphor tree.

In the meantime, seven years passed. When the third day of the third month came, although it was the Girls' Festival day, he asked his wife to prepare the grandest festive dishes for their only son. These were packed in seven-tiered lacquer boxes.

"My dear son, now take this set of lacquer boxes, packed with delicious foods, and go toward the east," the father said. "You will first come to a field of yellow rape blossom. After that you will come to a sweet, fragrant plum grove; then you will come to a pear orchard; and after passing that you will come to a peach orchard filled with pink flowers; all these flowers will make you pleased and happy. When you come to a hill, from where you will see the wide blue sea, you must stop to rest and wait for us. We will be coming soon after you."

The son thought this was just one of the ways to celebrate the festival. So without much thought he went out of the house carrying the seven-tiered lacquer boxes, walking along the paths his father had told him about. It was like a dream for him to walk through the sea of yellow rape flowers, and those fragrant orchards. He finally came to a hill, where he stopped to rest and wait for his parents.

"Ah, this is the wide open sea. But I'm getting hungry," the boy said and began to open the lacquer boxes. But as he began to eat, the silence of the sea was suddenly broken, and a weird sea monster slowly emerged from the water. In another moment the monster jumped over the beach and sat beside the boy.

"What are you eating? Hmm, they look delicious, let me have some," the monster said and began to take the food from the lacquer boxes. The food was so good that the monster devoured everything.

"Ah, what a feast!" the monster cried out. "It was so good that I've forgotten all about you. It was you I came here to eat, but now that my stomach is full, I'll spare your life. In fact, for all the delicacies I'll prolong your life to eighty-eight years." Then the monster jumped into the sea and disappeared, according to an old story, which all parents still tell to their children in that part of Nagasaki Prefecture.

The beautiful
Lake Tazawa

A long time ago there was an honest man called
Sannojo living deep in the mountains of the northern Province of Ugo (present Akita Prefecture). He
and his wife lived without any worries about their
livelihood, as he was always busy cutting down
trees and making charcoal for the villagers down
in the valley.

However, they were lonesome because they had
no children. So they went to all the temples and
shrines in the district to pray to the gods and the
Great Buddha that they might be blessed with a
child. Their prayers were answered, in the Year of
the Dragon, when the wife bore a baby girl. They
named her Tatsuko, in tribute to the Year of the
Dragon.

The baby was fondly and most lovingly reared
by Sannojo and his wife, and in time grew up to
be the most beautiful maiden in the entire prov-

ince. All the young men of the province and even from other places came to woo her. While she was in her prime, her father died. But her mother survived to look after her.

One day while Tatsuko was admiring her own beauty, she happened to see her aged mother, and thought, "Many years from now I, too, must become old, and look as haggard as my old mother. No, that I could never tolerate." And so she went to the temple of the venerable Goddess of Mercy to consult and to be taught how she could retain her beauty perpetually. And she prayed to the Goddess day and night for twenty-one days asking that her beauty might last forever. On the night of the twenty-first day, her prayer was answered by the Goddess of Mercy: "However earnestly you may pray, your request cannot be attained. It is almost hopeless to ask me."

"My dearest Goddess, I understand you perfectly well, but I still believe that there must be some means whereby I can retain my beauty eternally."

"Tatsuko, you are too selfish. If you do not mind losing yourself for your beauty, there is a way, but it is too mean," the Goddess warned her.

By this time Tatsuko could not think of anything else. And so she immediately replied that whatever might happen to her, she would not regret it, and that she would like to retain her beauty perpetually.

"You will not repent?" the Goddess asked to confirm her wish.

"Yes, my dear Goddess, I shall not repent. I shall endure any hardship to attain it," Tatsuko pledged.

"If you are so determined, then climb up this mountain northward until you come to a sparkling spring. If you drink the water of the spring, your wish will come true. But it will be too late for you to repent after that," the kindly Goddess of Mercy said very sorrowfully, while stroking her fluffy hair mercifully, and disappeared.

That winter was a long one for Tatsuko, because she had to wait until spring in order to go into the snow-covered mountains. When spring finally came Tatsuko and her girl friends started for the mountains to pick the budding sprouts of ferns (eaten as relishes by the people).

The girls ran all over the mountains gleefully to pick the budding sprouts, but Tatsuko simply ignored them and kept climbing in quest of the sparkling spring. When at last she came to the long-sought-after spring, she felt so thirsty that she knelt down and began to quench her thirst. It was sweet, so she drank more, and the more she drank the more thirsty she felt. In time she drank so much that she felt well satisfied and lay down on the ground and fell into a deep slumber.

When she woke up, it was in the midst of a rainstorm. The place where she had been sleeping was already filled with rainwater, and the entire region had become a large pool of water like a lake surrounded by verdant hills.

Meanwhile, when Tatsuko's mother heard that her daughter had not returned from the mountains, she lost no time and hurried up the mountain paths with a torch in her hand in search of her. At length she came upon a lake, which she had not seen before, and decided to rest.

While she was resting there by the lakeside, she thought she should call Tatsuko, and cried out as loud as she could over the surface of the lake.

"Tatsuko! Tatsuko! Tatsuko!"

Her pitiful cries spread swiftly over the lake, and then echoed back from the other side. Soon she saw something quivering in the water near her. Then she looked down into the water, and with the light of her torch she perceived her beautiful daughter smiling joyously at her.

"Why, Tatsuko! What are you doing there?" the mother cried out in astonishment, and took a step into the water to reach her.

"No, Mother! Do not come further. It was my fervent wish. The Goddess of Mercy has given me my perpetual beauty, and here I am now. Please come and see me whenever you want to talk to me," Tatsuko said. And she kept on smiling ever so pleasantly at her mother.

Tatsuko's mother saw that although she had retained her beautiful features, her body had changed to a dragon's. She watched her daughter swimming away from her into the depths of the lake until the last bit of her torch burned out. The blackened torch then fell into the lake and became a trout.

The lake has hence come to be known as Lake Tazawa. And the trout in the lake has also become famous as the token of the everlasting love shown by Tatsuko's mother, who was said to have spent the rest of her life by the lakeside with her pitiful but beloved daughter.

Tatsuko's romance

WHEN the cold wintry wind begins to sweep down from the surrounding mountains over the peaceful surface of the picturesque Lake Tazawa, the wild ducks come to the lake to take refuge from the severe northern winter. Tatsuko, the dragon spirit of this mountain lake, always waited for the wild ducks to hear good news from different parts of the country. It was her utmost pleasure to listen to their tales. One year the wild ducks told her about Hachiro-Taro, now living in Hachiro-gata, on the Japan Sea coast in the same province. She was very much interested in Hachiro-Taro, because he was, like Tatsuko herself, transformed from human form. Besides, the wild ducks told her that he was strong and handsome, and possessed such a magnanimous heart that everybody loved him.

When the snow of the mountains began to melt, the wild ducks also began to fly away to the north. "If you happen to pass by Lake Hachiro-gata ..." Tatsuko called after them.

"Yes, yes. We know exactly what you want, and we'll surely tell Hachiro-Taro about you," the wild ducks said and flew away to the northern lands.

Tatsuko had to wait for another long year to hear what tidings she could get of Hachiro-Taro the following winter, when the wild ducks returned to her lake. According to the wild ducks the winter at Hachiro-gata was severe. It was often struck by blinding blizzards from the Japan Sea and during the long winter months the surface of the lake was for the most part frozen.

When Tatsuko heard about the severe time Hachiro-Taro had to endure, she became anxious and consulted the wild ducks. "Do you think it would be possible for Hachiro-Taro to come to Lake Tazawa during the bleak winter months?"

The wild ducks thought it was a wise plan, because, "When we told him about you he was also very much interested in meeting you. If you invite him, he will surely come here," they suggested.

The following year when the northern winds began to blow, Tatsuko's heart also began to beat faster than before, thinking about Hachiro-Taro,

who was sure to come. One day while she was resting in a quiet inlet of her lake, she began to hear a
heavy rustling noise coming down from the hills
overlooking the lake. It was Hachiro-Taro in the guise
of a handsome young man, but when he plunged into
the lake he was changed into a male dragon.

Tatsuko watched him all the time from the inlet,
and although she was shy, she finally approached
him and welcomed him cordially.

"What a beautiful lake, you have, compared with
my desolate pool; the surrounding hills are splendid,

the water reflecting the serene scenery is so clear, and the spirit of this lake is wonderfully charming," Hachiro-Taro said in amazement at the beauty of Lake Tazawa.

When Tatsuko heard all the praising words from Hachiro-Taro, whom she had been hoping for years to meet, she felt almost awestricken. But at the same time she felt so shy that she could not express her happy feelings. And yet the two understood each other and soon felt as if they had known each other for a long time.

"My abode, as you know, is a rough one. In midwinter when the wild blizzard comes from the sea, the lake is frozen overnight, and when the moon gets thin and disappears, my lake gets frozen until the moon becomes full. Here everything is so warm and beautiful and I feel so fortunate," Hachiro-Taro continued to praise Tatsuko's lake.

"You are always welcome, and please stay here as long as you wish, as my guest," Tatsuko said.

In the meantime winter passed and spring came. The snow began to melt and new sprouts began to appear in the trees of the surrounding forests. While Hachiro-Taro and Tatsuko were enjoying their days, one day he said, "It's spring and I must return to my lake by the sea," and thanked Tatsuko warmly for the long sojourn during the comfortable winter months there.

When Tatsuko heard him, she felt lonesome and sad. "My dear Hachiro, if you do not mind, you can stay here with me as long as you please. I'd rather have you stay here all the days of the year. It is my fervent wish."

"If it is possible I'd like to do that. But as the Gongen deity has so kindly given me the lake by the sea, after I was driven out of Lake Towada, I must go back and look after it."

"Then, will you come here again this year-end to spend the winter with me?" she pleaded.

"Yes, I will be very glad to return here again, when the wild ducks and geese begin to come from the north."

Thereafter, Hachiro-Taro made it a yearly custom to spend the winter in the beautiful Lake Tazawa with the ever lovable Tatsuko, so an old Akita tale still tells us. It is also said that the water of Lake Tazawa never gets frozen because of the warm love of the two romantic dragon spirits living there.

YOHAN'S
HELP YOURSELF
SERIES

INSTANT JAPANESE

¥1000 A short introduction to
a unique language ; the phrases
you'll want to know and use,
in a form which you'll enjoy and
remember. Convenient pocket
size.

INSTANT JAPAN

¥1000 A companion volume
to *Instant Japanese,* giving a
once-over-lightly resumé of
sights to see and what to do
and why Japan is what it is and
how it happened

YOHAN
ENGLISH-JAPANESE
JAPANESE-ENGLISH
DICTIONARY

¥2000

An English-Japanese, Japa-
nese-English Pocket Dictionary
in One Concise Volume, Sim-
ulated Leather Binding
5,140 most useful words from
English to Japanese
6,396 most useful words from
Japanese to English
7cm. × 11cm., 528pp.

These prices exclude the consumption tax.